3,98

THE GREATEST REAL ESTATE BOOK IN THE WORLD

THE GREATEST REAL ESTATE BOOK IN THE WORLD

THE WAY TO MAKE A FORTUNE IN THE '80s

ROBERT A. STLOUKAL

Times BOOKS

Published by TIMES BOOKS, a division of
Quadrangle/The New York Times Book Co., Inc.
Three Park Avenue, New York, N.Y. 10016

Published simultaneously in Canada by
Fitzhenry & Whiteside, Ltd., Toronto

Library of Congress Cataloging in Publication Data

Stloukal, Robert A
  The greatest real estate book in the world.

  Bibliography: p. 237
  Includes index.
1. Real estate investment. I. Title.
HD1375.S745   332.6′324   79-66846
ISBN: 0-5l7-350033

Manufactured in the United States of America

For my wife, Theresa,
and my daughter, Lara.

ACKNOWLEDGMENTS

Expressing gratitude is civilized and just. It also takes the place of money. In this spirit, I confess a shameless reliance on Ron Aiello, Brian Ashe, Kenne Bristol, Mike Callahan, Phil Caputo, Bob Dickey, Bob Harring, Carl Kupfer, Marcus Ladd, Don Langford, Jack Napoli and Don Neuses. In addition to their expertise, I am further ennobled by their friendship. Their willingness to listen to the difficulties involved may require a new definition of the word "endurance."

I would also like to express a special thanks to my typists, Jean Boyce, Denise Jansky, Mary Reis and Ellen V. Stloukal who, if they ever tire of typing, have promising careers in decrypting.

My mother is like all of our mothers. They understand everything about us and they understand nothing about us. Their willingness to improve on the accident of birth is, for motherhood, a universal trait. It is our fault that they never succeed. We are all in some way disreputable only because we do not have our mother's eyes.

As for my wife, she has been invaluable to me as typist, companion, lover, saint, realist, grammarian, mother, cook, motivator, wailing wall and that's enough for now.

CONTENTS

THE GREATEST REAL ESTATE BOOK IN THE WORLD

CHAPTER *1*

WEALTH

To be poor without murmuring is difficult.
To be rich without being proud is easy.

—Confucius

Wealth buys freedom, banishes insecurity, creates power, guarantees respectability, allows leisure for philosophy, implements lofty ideals, makes easy a composure necessary for good manners, provides an environment from which happiness and fulfillment may develop, excuses folly, relieves anxiety in that most graceless of times—old age—and, when coupled with clout, lands an ambassadorship. The only shame of wealth is the tendency of the rich to keep secret or frustrate in others its method. This tendency comes naturally to the wealthy as they can prove their wealth only by ensuring that most of their brethren aren't. Due to inflation, higher taxation, government over-regulation and industrial concentration, the door to the wealth club has become somewhat ajar. But, believe me, it is by no means locked. This only means that a certain amount of gate crashing is now necessary. Once you're in, acceptability is automatic.

Money is not the root of all evil, but its absence is. Furthermore, poverty* is not an aide to elegance, does nothing for your self-esteem, is wrongly viewed as a manifestation of stupidity and forces you to wear polyester suits. The only similarity between wealth and poverty is that both tend to be hereditary.

By reading, understanding and putting into effect the principles of this book, you will be able to enjoy the advantages of wealth and evade the disadvantages of poverty, to say nothing of your eventual ability to discern the difference between beluga and lumpfish.

THE LIMITS OF WEALTH

This book will not make you happy. It will only make you rich. It will not cure your bad habits, but only raise them to the status of idiosyncrasies. It won't reconcile a bad marriage, restore your health or bring about world peace. The chances are it won't even solve your money problems! Higher personal incomes invariably

---

*I use a rather liberal definition of poverty. It includes not only the truly poor, but the middle-income groups. In short, most of the country.

seek out still higher personal expenses. The only serious problem wealth can contend with is poverty.

In addition, it is widely known that sudden wealth frequently turns the recipient's head. Meanness, vindictiveness, pettiness or foolishness, pride and debauchery may soon follow.

THE SELF-GENERATING
CHARACTERISTIC OF WEALTH

Just as there is no such thing as a little foreplay, so there is no such thing as a little wealth. The first $200,000 is always the hardest. This is the "sweat money" without which rapid, exponential financial growth becomes impossible. Remember Harry Truman's "A banker is someone who will loan you all the money you want if you can prove to him you don't need it." In an inflationary age, without the ability to borrow big and under favorable terms, true financial security becomes elusive.

We've all heard for too long the common plaint of the loser, "If only five years ago I had invested in _____ I'd be a rich man today." The chances are he didn't have the money, confidence or both to invest in _____ five years ago. This book will give you the money in a shorter time than you may think and, I hope, the confidence to act.

If you don't want success, you'll never get it. There are numerous road shows (they're expensive) whose sole function is to instill motivation. Instilling desire without spelling out a method is like being marooned on a desert island with your bowling team. You need a vehicle to success and real estate is and has been the best game in town.

THE NONESSENTIALS

The method discussed in this book discounts or ignores special advantages the reader may have on his road to wealth. Luck, genius, influence or a substantial inheritance are ignored due to the very selective nature of fate. You don't really believe a rich uncle is going to pimp you into a percentage job of selling jets to the Saudis. An unnatural work lust is discounted as (a) it is no longer very important and (b) it's bad for your health. Likewise, a willingness to "stick it" to family, friends and business associates is not considered, although it a) may be a behavioral necessity, it b) may also be bad for your health. And, finally, a willingness to commit a felony is ignored because jails aren't what they used to be. If, however, you have any of these edges—*use them.*

Of all the edges the reader may possess, education is the most useless. While a trained mind enables you to see all the advantages of a particular course of action, it also enables you to envision all the pitfalls. A dwelling on the latter soon reduces you to inaction. Economic trophies are bestowed only on the doers not the meditators. In short, the educated think too much. I hope this answers your question of why all your half-wit high school classmates are now driving Mercedes.

WEALTH AS A TRICK

Acquiring wealth is a trick like belching on cue and not a pendant dangling from genius. This trick is instinctive in a few, but for most (if it is to be mastered at all) it must be learned.

My sixth-grade friend Artie Konopasek was an instinctive belcher. His tone, volume and timing were masterful. However, what elevated his craft from a disgusting pastime to an art form was his ability to string them in series. A remembrance of those long-ago-heard arpeggios still warms. I finally learned the trick at the age of 25, but by that time the whimsy of it all was lost forever.

WHEN TO BEGIN

In old age you are considered venerable and wise or senile and burdensome in direct proportion to your estate. With this in mind, and understanding that middle age tends to impart an extreme sense of caution, the time to begin is *now!* Don't begin thinking about it NOW. Begin doing something about it *now.* Too many flawless financial transactions have taken place only in one's fantasies. Keep in mind that a two-flat apartment building in Bayonne has a greater cash flow than a skyscraper in Utopia. For me, Samuel Johnson forever defined the nature of genius with "A genius is someone who successfully puts into effect an idea you once had but discarded."

Here's another good reason for acting now. The era of opportunity may soon be over. Among our leaders (politicians, bureaucrats, judges, intellectuals, et al.), the dominant mood is one of economic leveling. This *Zeitgeist* has been gathering steam for quite a while and seems to be the wave of the future. They implement these leveling desires through a vindictive tax policy, over-regulation, irrational court decisions, foolish monetary policy and a general antibusiness, antiwealth behavior. I strongly suspect that the motive of our leaders is not to improve the lot of the poor, but rather to punish the successful. This leveling process will be complete once everyone is forced to endure a marginal economic existence. Poverty is, for you, dependence, and for them, power.

Finally, don't wait for everything to be perfect before you start. There is always an excuse not to act. This is an imperfect world and all the stars will never be in order.

ETHICS/LEGALITY

Until recent years, ethics and legality have fellow-traveled through our nation's history. However, we are now living in an age in which the term "law abiding" does not automatically confer civility or fairness. It only signifies that you are not currently in jail. The judges, enactors, implementors, exemplars, cheerleaders, and advocates of our laws and mores have long ago blasted off from our world of common sense. They have been made positively giddy in the transit knowing that their levitating factor is an endless series of noble causes. Although their attempts to improve things nearly always have the exact opposite effect, they are never discouraged. Space gives everyone a different perspective.

Those of us who are earthbound must rely on common sense and the golden rule (both of which are being outdistanced by the law) to govern our social and economic behavior. A sense of personal guilt may now be the only true determinant of wrongdoing.

Let's face it, a private sense of the law or morality is not the ideal but it's the only rational, coherent and understandable yardstick left to earth creatures. If it is true that behind every great fortune there is a great crime, may yours be only misdemeanors.

PUBLIC FIGURES AS MODELS

The reader is cautioned against looking toward many of our country's more visible brothers for inspiration, guidance or help. These "visibles," among them politicians, intellectuals and various other uplifters, are, for the most part, salesmen. Their only product line is *guilt* of which they have an unlimited inventory and the American people an insatiable demand.

The most dangerous of these "visibles" is the intellectual as he is the controller of the others. His dominance over many movie stars, politicians, clergymen, students, bureaucrats and various other causemongers puts him in a highly leveraged position.

I do not know how one becomes an intellectual, but I can tell you how not to become one. Few modern intellectuals have ever made a nickel, consulted the White House, written a book or achieved tenure by saying anything approaching common sense. They do not deal in the world of fact or reality, but specialize in the blabbermouth arts of diction and demagoguery. These musings, mostly nonsense, are soon elevated to national dogma. This dogma is nearly always socialist in nature and the trouble with socialism is that, sooner or later, it leads to murder.*

I suppose a strong, prosperous and ascendant nation can afford these clever house pets; indeed, a democratic one must. However, their influence corrodes and has corroded to a point that their prophecy of living with diminishing expectation is becoming true. It has never occurred to these loony tunes that they can survive

---

*I refuse to trivialize a book on real estate with a long-winded discussion of mass murder; however, international socialism's body count in this century is in excess of 50,000,000. Most of these corpses came from the middle class—SORRY.

only off the tailings of the productive classes. They are unable to understand that their purpose is solely for our amusement and for a few useful insights which, in all cases, must be amended in order to conform with reality.

As for bureaucrats, these cranks had the wisdom to get on the public payroll early in life. They have civil service to give them lifetime job security which allows them, unlike politicians, to be totally unresponsive to the public will. The most trivial piece of congressional legislation is soon expanded to the absurd by the zealous bureaucrat, thus giving to respectable legislation preposterous and unintended results. It is for this reason that our elected officials are becoming less influential as the power of the bureaucracy grows. I can foresee the day when the sole function of the politician will be to act as apologist for an all-powerful bureaucracy.

In a more charitable sense, no man can set up any other man as a model. All men, in time, disappoint. You have only God, mathematics and yourself as guarantors of your well-being.

WORKING FOR OTHERS

The principal drawback in working for others is that nobody wants to make you rich. The reasons are obvious: (1) the higher the employee's income, the less the employer's, (2) if the employee becomes too wealthy, he may no longer need his employer or, worse yet, become a competitor, and (3) should incremental raises put the employee in a lofty tax bracket, it won't be long before the employer finds two eager replacements to do the same job for one third the salary. This is to say nothing of dealing with the tedium, office politics and encrusted bureaucracy of many companies. There is no reason to become indignant about this. It's human nature. There is no long-term advantage in working for others.

REAL ESTATE AS THE IDEA

Real estate is the source of many of the world's great individual fortunes. It is also the principal vehicle by which all great fortunes are protected, enhanced and passed to succeeding generations. This is true now more than ever.

The uneven performances of the stock, bond and commodity markets have become too well known to be considered for long-term security. These investment methods rely too heavily on luck, rare inside knowledge or fortunes large enough to be manipulative.

Investment in art (including not only painting and sculpture, but rare coins, stamps, antiques, empty whiskey bottles, etc.) has become quite stylish; however, its potential is crippled by an inability to reckon with forgeries or the latest "hot flash" of the tastemaker. In addition, these investments require you to buy at retail and sell at wholesale. The customary mark up of these "investments" is 30 percent to 100 percent.

Even gold, voluptuous, unchangeable, decorative and barbaric, is only a store of wealth and not a producer of wealth. While the speculator may be temporarily rewarded with a price rise, he is frequently penalized with a subsequent price drop. These fluctuations are beyond the speculator's control as the price of gold is largely determined by the whim of national governments. In truth, gold never fluctuates, only national currencies do. The price of gold is nothing more than a direct measurement of the lunacy of national economic policy (inflation). The long-term future of gold is good only because our government's commitment to inflation is here to stay. However, gold, unlike real estate, is not subject to long-term financing and therefore is unleverageable. All that can be said about gold is that it is an excellent inflation hedge and therefore a respectable investment for the wealthy.

Only land, all beneath and all above, with its characteristics of fixed supply and durability, can act as both the cornerstone and producer of wealth. No other investment allows for more favorable long-term financing, and due to real estate's widely allocated ownership—read votes—offers better tax advantages.

In our age, mastering the trick of wealth has as its first step an understanding of the dominant economic fact of our time—*inflation*.

CHAPTER 2

INFLATION

If inflation makes us any richer, we'll starve to death.
—Author

*Y*our sociopolitical opinions from atomic energy to Zionism are your own, but continuing high inflation is a fact and it is you that must adapt it. There is no percentage in having your piety interfere with your technique. An understanding of inflation, its causes, effects, victims and beneficiaries is essential to everyone's well-being.

THE CAUSE OF INFLATION

The federal government, using the Federal Reserve System as its instrument, is the principal beneficiary and, therefore, the principal cause of inflation. Labor, big business and the farmer are the politician's usual scapegoats for inflation. These producing groups are only reacting to a government economic policy based on an ever-diminishing dollar. They ask for more for the sole purpose of staying even.

MONEY CREATION

The process of money creation begins with the federal government selling a security to an ever-accommodating Federal Reserve. The fed then issues a check, backed by nothing, which is then deposited in a commercial bank. Since our banks are required to keep in reserve only a fraction of what they lend or invest, the original amount of the government security is multiplied sevenfold. The sale of a $1 million security by the federal government to the Federal Reserve translates to $7 million "on the street."

The federal government thus cheapens our dollars by the simple expedient of making more of them. In spite of considerable gains in productivity by our nation's industry, the amount of goods and services has not been able to keep pace with the ever-increasing supply of money. Hence, more dollars seeking relatively fewer goods create higher prices.

Historically, no nation has been able to resist inflating its money. The princes of old relied on clipping, shaving or debasing the metal content of their coinage in order to finance their latest extravagance. This rather clumsy trick frequently produced short-term prosperity and long-term ruin. No breakthroughs were made in disguising government bankruptcy until the introduction of paper money in the late eighteenth century. The acceptability of this medium does not rely on the intrinsic value of its metal content, but rather on the intrinsic integrity of the politician. This subtlety, unlike a shrinking gold piece, always fools the trusting peasant.

The first 150 years of our nation's existence saw little or no change in the value of our money. However, what began as a New Deal expedient has developed into an undisciplined and unmanageable fiscal problem.

WAGE AND PRICE CONTROLS

War is economics on superheat and our Maginot line is wage and price controls, either voluntary or mandatory. These controls are the modern politician's favorite device for controlling inflation. Like most government tinkering in the affairs of free men, it is counterproductive. It actually contributes to inflation. The only benefit of wage and price controls goes to the politician as it serves to shift the blame of rising prices from himself to the labor and business communities.

No businessman or labor chieftain is startled to read in the newspaper that his industry is now subject to wage and price controls. All industries and unions maintain high-priced lobbyists in Washington whose job it is to predict such things. They know six months in advance of the actual implementation of controls and have plenty of time to "adjust" (raise) wages and prices to a level which will allow them to comfortably ride out the lid. This is inflationary. In addition to spurring inflation, wage and price controls in time cause scarcity, rationing, unemployment, black-market activity and, a personal irritant, queues.

INFLATION IS NOT A VICTIMLESS CRIME

The United States Government is the largest borrower in history. It is, therefore, in its interest to conduct itself in such a way as to favor borrowers at the expense of lenders. It is now necessary for inflation to continue its spiral so that the government may (a) "repay" its debts with cheapened dollars (repay less than it borrowed), b) increase its revenues by elevating its citizens to higher tax brackets (with a 10 percent rate of inflation, income tax revenues increase 16.5 percent) and (c) flood our banking system with enough monopoly money to keep interest rates artificially low (in most cases, below the rate of inflation). This is, for the politician, a more painless way to increase taxes.

The idea has never occurred to the modern politician (or bureaucrat) that his actions are destroying the very function of money, the principal function of money being a standard of value for both savings and debt repayment.

Any successful politician knows that a preoccupied public will swoon before a combination of physical presence, amiability and unfinanceable schemes. Repeated election victories in time add up to great influence and a network of power. Power is to the politician the only true goal.

Inflation's victims are not only the aged, the poor or anyone relying on a fixed income, but all those prudent, thrifty, trusting souls who have yet to fully understand the new rules of the game. These modern "rubes" whose savings accounts yield a 5.25 percent return in an 8 percent inflation year not only lose 2.75 percent in purchasing power on their savings but are made to endure the additional government grace note of being taxed on the 5.25 percent. The savings of these people make our continued economic expansion possible and should not be so mocked.

Inflation, our national vice, unlike democracy, our national virtue, is exportable. The central position of the dollar as the principal trading and reserve currency of the world makes its stability a worldwide concern.

The benchmark for determining government success or failure

in combating inflation is now 7 percent. With this standard, a 6.5 inflation year is considered a success! This is like awarding an A to a high school student for knowing 93.5 percent of the alphabet. In any other age, this would be considered preposterous.

GOVERNMENT REGULATION

Real estate, like so many other economic activities, has been dragged, kicking and screaming, into the government regulation sweatbox. A recent study has revealed that 20 to 25 percent of the cost of a new home can be attributable to federal and local government over-regulation. This partially explains why the median price of a new home increased from $27,600 in 1972 to $48,800 in 1977 and $61,000 by December of 1978! In many major markets, the increase in the cost of housing has doubled that of inflation. We can no longer take comfort in Will Rogers' "Be thankful we're not getting all the government we're paying for." In real estate, we are.

Federal, state and local authorities have many ways to increase the cost of new construction, which is then transferred to the resale market. Excessive minimum standards of lot and building size, with the resultant increased length of sanitary sewers, water pipes, curbs, gutters and street pavement, constitute one method. Other devices include construction overdesign, various environmental restrictions, land donations for schools and parks, interminable inspections at ever-increasing fees, much time wasted in waiting for various approvals, hundreds of man hours devoted to filling out forms and, of course, attorney's fees.

DIMINISHING RESOURCES

Good building lots, close to urban centers, are becoming increasingly scarce. This is primarily a function of population growth and only partially due to restrictive zoning. Lumber, along with other building materials, is suffering from the same scarcity. The cost of labor has shown a steady increase over the last 15 years. These trends will, of course, continue.

WHERE WILL IT ALL END?

The residential real estate market, with which I'm most familiar, has shown an 11.2 percent, 13.8 percent and 18 percent increase in the years 1975 thru 1977. The reader cannot help but ask himself whether homes will, sooner or later, be priced beyond the buyer's means and, thereby, depress the market. The answer is a roaring *"No"!*

Rising personal income somewhat sustains rising housing costs, but this is not the only answer. Sociological phenomena such as working wives and smaller families are also very important factors. But, for the future, the most important reason for sustained real estate growth will be financing. Any experienced real estate salesman can tell you *it's not the price of a home that keeps a buyer from purchasing. It is invariably the monthly payment.* There is nothing chiseled in marble which says the price of a home and the monthly payment are directly proportional. For example, increasing the mortgage term from 29 to 39 years would serve to reduce the monthly payment. Graduated monthly payment loans and variable interest rate loans are available on a limited basis and promise to be the wave of the future. These financing devices allow buyers to carry higher mortgages than with conventional financing.

Appreciation of existing homes has also been a major factor. The current homeowner (65 percent of American families) has been hedged in the housing market. If, for example, he has owned his present home for four years, he then has more than enough equity to "upgrade."

The recent success of Proposition 13 in California, unlike surfing, is an idea exportable to the rest of the nation. Given the overwhelming public support of this bill and understanding that all politicians can be regarded as geniuses only in matters touching on their own survival, a national trend toward lower property taxes seems inevitable. As to what this means to Californians, let's take a $100,000 house with property taxes of $3,600. A 57 percent reduction in taxes reduces the tax bill by $1,692. This $1,692 savings reduces the homeowner's monthly tax payment by $141. This savings has the effect of expanding the market of future buyers and thus leads to a higher sales price. To put it another way, since a buyer typically is concerned only with his monthly payment, a $141 reduction in payments at current interest rates has the effect (on the buyer only) of reducing the cost of the home by $16,400.

A reduction in long-term capital gains taxes has recently gained considerable support. The United States has the highest maximum capital gains tax rate in the industrialized world and a reduction in this tax can result only in an increase in capital investment and, therefore, jobs. This is good news for the real estate investor as it can result only in an increase in demand.

And, finally, the home buyer's motives have changed in the last few years. Recent surveys have shown that the primary motive for buying a home is now investment and only secondarily utility. When investment is the primary motive, the buyer loses guilt in raising his housing budget. This tends to make the buyer seek higher-priced housing.

These factors should serve to sustain the real estate market for the foreseeable future.

However, if you insist, the years 1990 to 1995 may see a leveling off or decline in real estate prices. This is due to the fact that the cost of real estate is more a function of population than any other factor. The year 1965 was the first year in our history of zero population growth and this trend is continuing. Since the typical nest-building age is between twenty-five and thirty, the years 1990–95 may be critical. These nonbuyers will be nonbuying in this period resulting in a decrease in demand. To the real estate investor, these years are too far off to be considered the investable future.

If, however, you find continual soaring real estate prices disturbing, remember, even the Black Plague had the beneficial effect of bringing full employment to French doctors. Due to the federal government's irrevocable commitment to inflation, the day is forever gone for an individual to save his way to economic security. We are living in an age that considers thrift a vice (or at least stupid) and spending a virtue. By mortgaging real estate to the maximum, the smart investor can so position himself as to make inflation work for him.

While in the last ten years real estate appreciation has exceeded that of inflation (in many years doubled that of inflation) the reader is cautioned against believing this is to be forever true. Ultimately, real estate will settle on a more orderly rate of growth, consistent with or slightly higher than inflation. There is enough evidence to show that the national market has already normalized from the furious activity of 1975–78.

If 1979 is a cooling-off period (like 1969 and 1974), then 1980 promises to be a boom year (like 1970 and 1975) due to a pent-up demand.

Those who predict a real estate depression independent of a severe and prolonged national depression are off the mark. There is no historical argument for a severe real estate crash. The depression years of 1893–94, 1913–14 and 1920–21 had little effect on housing prices. The Great Depression, beginning in 1929, saw a drop in housing prices, but not nearly as much as any other form of investment. Since 1940, and in spite of many recessionary periods, housing prices have shown an uninterrupted climb.

The real estate market will pass through these cycles. I would be surprised if it didn't. The years 1969, 1974 and 1979 have been trough years. Given this five-year pattern, 1984 may also be critical. This is not scientific but it is precedent.

Real estate is a diverse investment and a bad year for single-family housing always results in a good year for the apartment owner. This assumes that everyone has to live somewhere. If home sales lag, apartment rentals (and rents) climb. Slow years also present opportunities for those with investable funds. The logic being the same as buying snow shovels in July.

The following chart will help to explain this chapter. We can see that the ambient inflation rate now hovers around 7 percent. The savings-account interest is not only less but subject to tax and the mortgage rate has shown a relentless climb.

Year	Savings-Account Yield	Mortgage Rate	Inflation
1960	3.5	5.85	1.5
1961	3.5	5.87	.7
1962	4	5.90	1.2
1963	4	5.84	1.6
1964	4	5.78	1.2
1965	4	5.74	1.9
1966	4	6.14	3.4
1967	4	6.33	3.0
1968	4	6.83	4.7
1969	4	7.66	6.1
1970	4.25	8.27	5.5
1971	4.25	7.59	3.4
1972	4.25	7.45	3.4
1973	5	7.95	8.8
1974	5.25	8.92	12.2
1975	5.25	8.75	7.0
1976	5.25	8.90	4.8
1977	5.25	8.5	7.0
1978	5.25	8.75	9.0
1979	5.5 est.	10.5 est.	15.2 est.

The table on page 20 indicates how a dollar or any multiple thereof grows over the years when compounded. For example, a $50,000 home, if it appreciates 8 percent for five years, would have a projected value of $50,000 × 1.47 or $73,500.

IN MEMORIAM
NICOLO DELANO PONZI
1714–59

Nicolo Ponzi was born into poverty in Santa Lucia della Chiesa on Candlemas Day, 1714. Even then, the world overlooked Santa Lucia, an arid, backwater village known only for the raising of olives and escape plans. Little is known of his early life; however, history does record Ponzi as living in Paris in the autumn of 1736. It seems he was then engaged in a business he called the "selling of dreams."

COMPOUND INTEREST

Year	3%	5%	6%	7%	8%	10%	12%	15%	20%
1	$1.03	$1.05	$1.06	$1.07	$1.08	$1.10	$1.12	$1.15	$1.20
2	1.06	1.10	1.12	1.14	1.17	1.21	1.25	1.32	1.44
3	1.09	1.16	1.19	1.23	1.26	1.33	1.40	1.52	1.73
4	1.13	1.22	1.26	1.31	1.36	1.46	1.57	1.75	2.07
5	1.16	1.28	1.34	1.40	1.47	1.61	1.76	2.01	2.49
6	1.19	1.34	1.42	1.50	1.59	1.77	1.97	2.31	2.99
7	1.23	1.41	1.50	1.61	1.71	1.95	2.21	2.66	3.58
8	1.27	1.48	1.59	1.72	1.85	2.14	2.48	3.06	4.30
9	1.30	1.55	1.69	1.84	2.00	2.36	2.77	3.52	5.16
10	1.34	1.63	1.79	1.97	2.16	2.59	3.11	4.05	6.19
11	1.38	1.71	1.90	2.10	2.33	2.85	3.48	4.65	7.43
12	1.43	1.80	2.01	2.25	2.52	3.14	3.90	5.35	8.91
13	1.47	1.89	2.13	2.41	2.72	3.45	4.36	6.15	10.70
14	1.51	1.98	2.26	2.58	2.94	3.80	4.88	7.08	12.84
15	1.56	2.08	2.40	2.76	3.17	4.18	5.47	8.14	15.41
20	1.80	2.65	3.21	3.87	4.66	6.72	9.65	16.37	38.34
25	2.09	3.39	4.29	5.43	6.85	10.83	17.00	32.92	95.40
30	2.43	4.32	5.74	7.61	10.06	17.45	29.96	66.21	237
35	2.81	5.52	7.69	10.68	14.79	28.10	52.80	133	591
40	3.26	7.04	10.29	14.98	21.72	45.26	93.05	267	1,469
50	4.38	11.47	18.42	29.47	46.90	117	289	1,083	9,100

His "business" consisted of coaxing his neighbors into joining a club, the only requirements being to (1) send one golden louis to the member at the top of a list and (2) solicit ten new members into doing the same. In two weeks time the new member would be senior and thereby collect his just due of 10,000 louis—enough in those days to properly outfit a count and three viscounts.

The success of Ponzi's enterprise soon reached the ear of a middle-ranking duchess. She joined and found herself in the unaccustomed position of being junior to a shoemaker from Toulouse, an itinerant tinsmith, an out-of-work magician from Beauvais and the Bishop of Chalons, among other unwashed.

Modern research points to the bishop as having altered the cycle in order to gain monetary advantage for the kingdom of God. But this is of little import. The true cause of Ponzi's demise resulted from the whoopings of the duchess to anyone in the French court who would listen. Her eruptions so distressed the mistress of the lord high chamberlain that she was forced to retire to her quarters with a severe case of the vapors. Well, it wasn't long before the chamberlain dispatched all the king's horses and all the king's men to bring Ponzi to justice. They did, and it is recorded that justice has rarely been so swift or so thorough.

Ponzi soon found himself spending his days in a dungeon fit only for the growing of mushrooms and without so much as a chirping sparrow for companionship.

Alas, alone and broken, poor Ponzi's heart gave out its last feeble pit-a-pat on the feast of St. Polycarp, 1759.

Sure, it's easy for us to say, "Ponzi, you should have leapfrogged the goddamned duchess into a more advantageous position," but this would be out of character for Ponzi. In his own gentle, principled way, he was a true believer in the equality of man.

And yet, life was not finished humiliating Ponzi. It was said at the time that Ponzi's wife, Eleanora, eloped with a respectable embalmer from Bastalacaca, Calabria, not so much for love as a fierce desire to forever change her infamous surname.

And how do we commemorate this salesman of hope, with

monuments, with statues, with anthems or feast days? No. Who tends the flame? Who encases the relics? No one.

His bones lie in an unmarked grave and his name is now used only as a word prefix with scheme. The words "Ponzi Scheme" are used to describe a lower species of bunco, the pyramiding variety which soon runs out of gullible recruits.

Is this the way a civilized people treat the memory of the founding father of the chain letter, bogus oil lease, New Deal, Fair Deal, New Frontier and Great Society? Is this the way we express our gratitude to the brains behind Keynesian economics, door-to-door franchise cosmetic empires, the credit-card industry, insurance swindle, commodity market, deficit spending and social security system? Is this the way we remember the progenitor of the Federal Reserve System and all its dependencies, stock market, pari-mutuel betting, state of the union addresses, Medicare, state lotteries and countless intrigues to follow? I should say not.

Ponzi did more to affect the way we live than a regiment of Albert Schweitzers or an entire galaxy of Rhodes scholars. No Great Helmsman, Sun King, Genius of Menlo Park or Great Emancipator is fit to hold his train. No assortment of generalissimos, martyrs, union chieftains or other men of destiny are eligible to dry-clean his tunic. Let a covey of popes and a carriage of archdukes kneel in mortification. Let every nation under the cross bestow upon him their highest honor. May he be festooned with every conceivable medal, cross, ribbon, garland, scapular, baldric, lavaliere, cockade, sash, garter, fez, ceremonial sword, laurel, golden key and aguillette. May a hundred enameled badges, depicting long-forgotten saints, decorate his statue. Let the world's potters turn out a mountain of limited-edition crockery in his honor. May we be deluged by an ocean of coins, stamps, medallions and whiskey bottles celebrating his image. On his birthday may every city and village blind us with a display of flags, pennants, bunting, confetti, placards, icons, lapel pins, streamers and bumper stickers, and may we be numbed by the sounding of all sirens, horns, whistles, gongs, bagpipes, carillons and fireworks.

That we do so is nothing more than simple justice.

We are living in Ponzi's world.

AMEN

CHAPTER *3*

*F*INANCING

O debt, where is thy sting.
—Anonymous

*J*ust as great wars are fought with other people's blood, so great fortunes are amassed with other people's money. Never before has the ease of using O.P.M. been so favorable. Our grandfathers had to save for years to pay cash or accept a small short-term mortgage for their homes. In our age, deferring a two-week Florida vacation is enough to have a down payment. It's true that interest rates were lower, 5 percent in the "old days" versus 9.75 percent at this writing. However, of all the factors considered for wise real estate investment, the interest rate is the least important. The length and amount of the mortgage and the degree of leverage are of overwhelming concern.

HIGH INTEREST RATES

Like so many other elements of real estate, the home mortgage interest rate is a relative figure. It is high or low only in relation to what it was two years ago or will be two years from now. The past decade has shown a steady rise in interest rates (from 6 percent to 10 percent), but an even greater rise in the cost of real estate. If you don't like paying 10 percent, you'll be outraged when you have to pay 12 percent. It's not the principal of the thing, it's the interest.

The buyer is not completely defenseless before what he considers high interest rates. In September of 1975, I bought a home with a 9.25 percent interest rate. By January of 1977, the VA interest rate had fallen to 8 percent. This 1.25 percent difference in rate was enough for me to refinance in spite of approximately $2,000 in closing costs.

A buyer may, on occasion, get a clause written into his mortgage that permits him to renegotiate his loan with little or no penalty if the rates drop.

THE BEST TIME TO BUY

The best time to buy is now. An eligible buyer should never put off purchasing in anticipation of a drop in the interest rate. The rate, of course, may drop but this rarely compensates the buyer for the rising cost of real estate.

	Year 1	Year 2	Year 3
Price of Home	$50,000	$55,000	$60,000
Interest Rate (30 yr.)	10%	9%	8.5%
Principal & Interest Payment	$439.00	$442.75	$461.40

LEVERAGE

Should you buy a home for $40,000 with a 20 percent down payment ($8,000) and sell it two years later for $56,000 (a typical situation), your return is 200 percent. A $16,000 profit expressed in terms of an $8,000 investment, not the $40,000 purchase price. The $32,000 mortgage is not your money. It's O.P.M., but your return is based as if it were. This is leverage.

These figures become more dramatic if your down payment was only 5 percent of the purchase price, an 800 percent return to be exact! *Now this is leverage.*

Seventy-two is a most interesting number for any investor. It's the number which, when divided by the percent of return on any investment, gives the number of years required to double your original purchase price. For example, a bond yielding 6 percent would require 12 years to double the investment (72 divided by 6). Translating this to real estate, a home bought for $50,000 with 10 percent down and assuming a 13 percent rate of appreciation will double in price in five and a half years, but remember your original investment wasn't $50,000 but $5,000. Your return in five and a half years is 1,000 percent!

CLOSING COSTS

Both buyer and seller incur certain closing costs in the transfer of real estate. Exactly what constitutes closing costs varies according to local custom. A survey charge, title expenses, recording fees, prepaid homeowner's insurance, bank service charges, appraisal, credit check, origination fee, discount points and legal fees are some of the items included as closing costs.

On the purchase of a $50,000 home, a buyer may pay $1,500 in closing costs, but remember the exact figure depends on time and place. Of all the elements that comprise closing costs, POINTS are the most mysterious.

A point equals 1 percent of the original loan amount. Therefore, the following transaction requiring a 2.5 percent service charge would equal $1,000.

$$\begin{array}{ll} \$50,000 & \text{Purchase price} \\ -\,10,000 & \text{Down payment} \\ \hline \$40,000 & \text{Original mortgage} \end{array}$$

$$\$40,000 \times 2.5\% = \$1,000$$

The lender charges points in order to bring its yield on your loan to the current money market level. It is a one-time, "up front" charge that the buyer can view as prepaid interest. The longer you own your home, the more these points are spread over the life of the loan, hence the less the true yield to the lender.

For figuring purposes, the lender assumes the life of their average loan will be eight years (the national average). Therefore, one point is equal to .125 percent increase in interest. If you sell your home in eight years, then a 10 percent, 2.5 point loan gives a true yield to the lender of 10.3125 percent. It is for this reason that no two borrowers of 10 percent money ever pay the exact *true* interest rate.

THE BANKER

All interactions with people are, properly speaking, "show biz." This is never more important than when asking for, say, $50,000 of the bank's money. While the banker will tolerate a certain lack of sophistication by the home buyer, he will never tolerate it from the real estate investor. Never is the old admonition of "Look British, Think Yiddish" more important.

Sloppy dress, speech or behavior do not beguile the loan officer. Likewise, showing up without an appointment and without a correctly filled out financial statement will diminish your chances of success.

The following is a good procedure to follow when applying for a loan:

1. Check at least 10 local banks for mortgage terms. Unless you are overdrawn, your own bank is a good place to start. Don't overlook the bank that handles large accounts for your company. If you have a friend in banking, don't overlook his ability to get you a "good deal."

2. Call on, say, Friday, and make an appointment with the mortgage loan officer for Tuesday.

3. On Monday, stop in the bank and pick up a financial statement form. (Make it two, you'll screw the first one up.)

4. Completely fill out this form. This not only tells the lender how solvent you are, but is used as the basis for the bank issuing a credit check. And remember, never, never, never misrepresent the facts when filling out this form, unless a) you can't get the loan without doing so and b) you have a reasonable chance of getting away with it.

5. Observe all standards of Western hygiene and be on time for the interview.

6. Keep in mind that the loan officer correctly views his position as that of devil's advocate. Be prepared to counter any objections he may have. For example, when buying a six-flat, the loan officer may ask you about the vacancy rate, the condition of the roof, heater, etc. Listen to him. He only wants to know if you know what you're doing. He may also bring up problems you may never have considered. The banker also acts as a wet blanket in order to avoid reproach should anything go wrong.

TYPES OF FINANCING

In so many cases, financing is as important to the investor as the building itself. An understanding of financing alternatives is basic to the real estate player.

VETERANS ADMINISTRATION LOAN

A VA loan is available to all those who have served in the military on active duty for more than six months (World War II and Korean War veterans need only three months active duty) and who have been discharged for any reason other than dishonorable. This loan is also available to unremarried widows of those who died in service and those currently on active duty for more than six months. No down payment is necessary up to $100,000. After $100,000, 25 percent of the difference between the VA appraised value and $100,000 is required (i.e., a building appraised and selling for $140,000 would require a $10,000 down payment).

Not too many years ago, a veteran was allowed to use his VA mortgage benefits only once in his lifetime (with a few exceptions). However, now, upon selling his first VA-mortgaged home, he may buy another using the same VA benefits.

In addition, the VA has raised, over the years, the maximum no-money-down loan amount from its original $8,000 to the present $100,000. This may allow an investor whose home is VA financed to buy another residence and rent his present home.

For example, if you bought your present home in 1967 for $50,000, which was then the maximum no-money-down loan and since the current maximum is $100,000, you are now entitled to buy another home for $50,000 with no down payment. This home must be your primary residence and should you decide to buy a home costing in excess of this amount, say $60,000, then, as before, you would be required to put down $2,500. This allows you to own two VA-financed properties concurrently; one is your principal residence and the other is rental property. Check with your local VA office for the exact dollar amount of your eligibility.

Not only homes but apartment buildings up to four units are

eligible for this type of financing. This loan is restricted to owner occupants, but the length of time you are required to live in the building is not specified.

ADVANTAGES

1. No down payment is necessary up to $100,000. This represents the ultimate in leverage.

2. Interest rates and points are less than conventional financing.

3. This loan is assumable at the original terms of the mortgage. This becomes very important as interest rates inch up. In a 10 percent mortgage market, a one-year-old VA loan written at 8 percent is quite attractive to any subsequent buyer. So attractive that he will, in all probability, be willing to pay more than the building is worth. In other words, he is buying favorable financing in addition to real estate. His closing costs are minimized by assuming the mortgage balance and terms of the original loan and he is not required to be a veteran.

4. No prepayment penalty can be charged for early retirement of the loan.

DISADVANTAGES

1. A VA loan requires the seller to pay a penalty to the lending institution. This penalty (called discount points) generally varies from 1 percent to 9 percent of the new loan. A $50,000 loan could conceivably require the seller to pay $3,000 to your lender that he wouldn't have to pay if you financed with a conventional bank loan. Therefore, the chances are you'll have to pay full asking price for the building (or more). The purpose of discount points is to restore the lender's composure after having made a loan at a rate considerably less than market.

2. VA loans are not available for many types of real estate, such as vacant land, vacation property, homes requiring a considerable amount of repair and many, but not all, town houses and condominiums.

3. The VA interest rate is set by the Veterans Administration.

It is adjusted from time to time and if you are unfortunate enough to sign a contract on February 1 to close on March 15 and if the VA raises its interest rate on March 14 you pay the new (higher) rate. However, the new rate will still be less than available elsewhere and rarely jumps more than .5 percent.

Once you own the home, the interest rate remains constant throughout the term of the mortgage.

It is important to note that the Veterans Administration is not a lending institution but serves only to guarantee whoever makes the loan that the buyer will not default. As an afterthought, it is also worth noting that the federal government has yet to put war on a performance basis. Yes, you're still eligible if you served in the one we lost.

FEDERAL HOUSING ADMINISTRATION LOAN

Like the VA, the FHA is not a lending institution, but only insures whoever makes the loan against loss. At any one time the interest rate of both is the same. Both programs have as their goal a more widespread ownership of real estate, and both types of loans can be assumed by a future buyer. Here the similarity stops. The following are the important differences:

1. Anyone is eligible.
2. A small down payment is required.
3. The maximum mortgage amount is less.
4. A number of different financing programs are available under FHA, making it more flexible.

FHA 203b is the FHA's basic home mortgage plan. These 30-year loans have the following maximum mortgage amounts for owner-occupied homes or apartment buildings:

(a) Single-family residence $60,000
(b) Two–three-family building $65,000
(c) Four-unit building $75,000

The down payment is 3 percent of the first $25,000 of mortgage and 5 percent thereafter. The down payment on a $50,000 home would then be $2,000.

$$
\begin{array}{rcl}
3\% \times \$25,000 = & \$ \ 750 \\
+ \ 5\% \times \$25,000 = & \underline{1,250} \\
& \$2,000
\end{array}
$$

In some cases, an FHA loan can be had with a lesser down payment. You can check with your local FHA office or mortgage banker to see if you qualify.

LAND CONTRACT

This method of financing amounts to the seller totally or partially financing the buyer. It's a great way to finance but few sellers are in a position to act as banker. The ideal seller in a land contract sale (a) does not need his equity in order to buy his next home and (b) is willing to take his profits from the sale of his building in installments spread out over years in order to gain important capital gains tax advantages.

The advantages to the buyer are (a) he can generally get an interest rate 1 or 2 percent below that of any lending institution, (b) he may deduct the interest and taxes as if the title were in his own name and (c) he can frequently put a lesser down payment than normally required by a lender.

The seller enjoys minimal risk in that the buyer's mortgage is a lien on the property and, should the buyer default, the worst that can happen to him is he gets his building back, which in the interim has continued to appreciate. It is important that both the buyer and seller in this type of agreement have attorneys. These agreements get quite complex, particularly in regard to what constitutes a default. However, as any attorney can tell you, there is a lot of money to be made in complexity.

CONVENTIONAL MORTGAGES

20 percent Down Payment. If there is such a thing as a standard loan, this is it. Lenders feel quite comfortable with a 20 percent down payment as this is enough equity to incur the costs of dispossessing the buyer in the event of a default. These costs include attorneys' fees, building repairs, if necessary, and sales commissions. No appreciable deduction in interest rate is to be found in putting more than 20 percent down and never enough to compensate the investor for his loss of leverage. This is a good loan for the investor because (a) it is offered at the lowest conventional loan rate and (b) it's easy to get. It may also be the only loan you can get.

Less Than 20 percent Down Payment. These loans are available in most money markets but may disappear altogether when money is "tight." This type of loan is available principally to owner occupants, but may be given on a limited basis to owners who do not live on the premises. Due to the higher risk involved, the interest rates are .25 percent to .5 percent higher. In addition, the borrower is frequently required to pay an additional .25 percent of private mortgage insurance. This insures the lender against your defaulting and has the curious effect of the borrower insuring his own virtue.

ASSUMPTIONS

All FHA and VA loans are, by law, assumable under the existing conditions of the loan. For example, a VA loan given five years ago at 7.5 percent for 30 years can now be assumed by a buyer, giving the seller the difference between the selling price of the home and the current mortgage balance. The interest rate to the new buyer remains the same (7.5 percent) and the term remaining is 25 years. This type of financing has the additional advantage of minimizing the closing costs.

FHA (245) GRADUATED PAYMENT LOANS

This is a very new concept in mortgaging. This type of loan is designed to accommodate the young, first-home buyer. The buyer's monthly payment rises each year for a specified number of years. The underlying logic in the lender making this type of loan is that due to inflation and upward mobility, the borrower's income can be expected to rise. This rise in income can then be used to make higher payments.

The FHA has five different graduated payment programs and one may be right for you.

> *Plan I.* Monthly mortgage payments increase at 2.5 percent each year for 5 years.
> *Plan II.* Monthly mortgage payments increase at 5 percent for 5 years.
> *Plan III.* Monthly mortgage payments increase at 7.5 percent each year for 5 years.
> *Plan IV.* Monthly mortgage payments increase at 2 percent for 10 years.
> *Plan V.* Monthly mortgage payments increase at 3 percent for 10 years.

During each year the payments will remain the same, and starting at the sixth or eleventh year the payment will be the same for the remaining term of the loan.

Plan III is the fastest track and therefore the most commonly used.

The down payment is higher with a G.P.M. loan. How much higher depends on which plan you choose, but if we take Plan III and use it to buy a $50,000 house, the down payment would be approximately $4,000 as opposed to $2,000 if you bought the home using the basic FHA 203b loan.

It is important to note that the borrower's payments during the initial period of the loan are less than interest only. The difference between the interest-only payment and what the borrower actually pays is called "negative amortization" and this is tacked on to your outstanding mortgage balance. In other words, you pay it someday.

This is a good loan for a young, first-home buyer as it is limited to owner occupants of single-family homes. Like all other FHA and VA loans, it is assumable by a future buyer and the owner may convert at any time to more conventional financing.

As of January 1, 1979, banks and savings and loan associations have been allowed to grant their own variation of the FHA-sponsored G.P.M. loan. Their version is quite similar to the FHA's and while an evaluation of their effect on the loan market is, at this time, impossible, the following differences occur:

1. Slightly higher down payment.
2. Probably a higher interest rate.
3. The seller does not pay discount points which may allow you to buy at a lesser price.
4. More flexibility within the Plan I–V guidelines.

VARIABLE RATE MORTGAGES (V.R.M.)

V.R.M.s are currently allowed only in California, but I expect this mortgage option to be available in all states in the near future.

These loans, while issued at current interest rates, may vary from year to year according to changes in the money market. The interest rate can go up or down, thus changing your mortgage payment. This loan is safer than you may think as there are limits to interest rate movements. Interest rates may not move up or down more than .5 percent per year or increase more than 2.5 percent during the life of the loan.

Upon notification of a rate increase, the buyer has the option of extending the loan maturity to a maximum of one third of the original loan term (i.e., a 30-year mortgage can be changed to a 40-year mortgage). This is a good loan to get if you feel interest rates are too high and expect them to drop. It is also a way of reducing your payments by getting an otherwise unobtainable 40-year mortgage.

The roll-over mortgage is a subspecies of the V.R.M. With this type of loan, the lender and borrower renegotiate interest rates every five years. Borrowers in California are currently favoring the roll-over to the V.R.M.

REVERSE ANNUITY MORTGAGE (R.A.M.)

The R.A.M. loan has also been made universally available as of January 1, 1979. While it is an outstanding idea, it's not for everyone. It is perfectly suited to those who:

1. Are or soon will be retired.
2. Have no major assets other than substantial equity in their homes.
3. Must rely solely on social security to meet their living expenses.

A reverse annuity mortgage may be the solution to this unenviable position. In the past, retirees have sold their homes and invested the proceeds in order to lead a comfortable retirement. But they became apartment dwellers subject to ever-increasing rents and lost all the psychological and economic (appreciation) advantages of home ownership. A R.A.M. allows the owner to retain ownership of his home and receive a check every month. The lender does this by gradually reducing the equity in the home. This type of loan becomes due either upon a specific date or when a specific event occurs, such as the sale of the home or the death of the borrower.

ADVANTAGES

1. You not only retain ownership of your home, but get to spend half or more of the equity during your lifetime.
2. If you have the good fortune of dying during the term of this loan, you can consider all the money you received as an interest-free gift. This may be the only time in your life that you get something for nothing. Unfortunately, your heirs don't look at it this way since, upon your death, your home is sold and only then does the lender collect the principal and interest on the balance of its mortgage to you. It's important to note that you're not cheating your heirs, but only leaving them less and in no case can

they inherit a debt. If you still feel guilty about this, ask yourself how much money they ever left you.

3. You may sell your home anytime you wish or you may pay off the loan, without penalty.

4. The lender's monthly payment to you does not affect your social security eligibility and is tax free. If you were to leave this money to your heirs, it would be subject to inheritance tax.

The lender sends you a monthly check for the principal only and in reverse order of the amortization schedule. In other words, on a 15-year R.A.M., your first month's check is the highest, let's say $300, and your last check is the lowest, say $30. Should you live past 80 and have outlived your 15-year R.A.M., the possibility exists that you could apply for another 10-year R.A.M. due to the fact that your home may have by then shown considerable appreciation. If you live past 90, sell and celebrate.

THE CHICAGO PLAN

At this writing, the Chicago Plan method of financing is available only to residents of Chicago; however, I see a bright national future for this or similar types of financing. This method consisted of the city of Chicago issuing $100,000,000 in tax-free municipal bonds. A tax-free yield of 7.5 percent made these bonds quite attractive to the investor and they were sold without difficulty. These funds were then made available to local lenders for home mortgages. Any single-family, multiple dwelling or condominium within the city limits was eligible for this type of financing. The maximum mortgage amount was $40,000 for up to 29 years. The interest rate was 7.99 percent (in a 10 percent market) and rehabilitation loans were given under the same terms.

This rather complex lending scheme made everyone happy. The buyer was happy to get a loan approximately 2 percent under the prevailing rate. The bond investor received a 7.5 percent return (tax free) which, if he is in the higher tax brackets, may equal a 12–15 percent return. The city was not only happy with the favorable publicity, but due to the rehabilitation loans that were made was able to increase its tax collections through the many property improvements.

THE VIRTUES OF THE CHICAGO PLAN

This program helped the middle- and lower-income groups afford housing in Chicago which they otherwise might not be able to afford. In addition, the role played by the city of Chicago was a passive one. This loan does not involve any government subsidy. Chicago's only role was to enable free market forces to respond to a need.

THE FUTURE OF THE NEW LENDING CONCEPTS

The standard fixed-rate, fixed-payment, fixed-term mortgage is and will continue to become less important to the buyer. Escalating payment loans (G.P.M.s or V.R.M.s), loans based on the Chicago Plan formulas or loans made in excess of 30 years are part of the future. This is particularly true for the first-home buyer as conventional loans may make the initial monthly payments beyond his means.

Lenders are making these adjustments in order to sustain their loan market, but many buyers must also adjust to current conditions. A principal motive for buying a home is the security it affords. Nothing offers more security than predictable, constant payments, and an escalating payment loan, while limited, does not provide this. The first-home buyer may have to make this compromise.

BANKRUPTCY

A past bankruptcy may or may not prohibit a buyer from getting a mortgage loan. A bankruptcy resulting from a business failure, lawsuit or high medical expenses is viewed more charitably by the lender than a bankruptcy resulting from an inability to restrain one's buying in a consumer society. In other words, you are either a swashbuckling, risk-taking, high-flying doer that happened to run into bad luck or a "mooch" unable to understand that the negative difference between cash inflow and cash outflow cannot be sustained forever.

In either case, a period of at least one year will have to have elapsed between bankruptcy and applying for a loan. This allows the lender to judge how you have handled your obligations from this point. It is a good idea to re-establish credit as soon after the bankruptcy as possible and keep the accounts up to date. The borrowers will be required to give written, detailed explanation for the bankruptcy. The borrower shouldn't treat this as an exercise in humiliation, but rather as an opportunity to display creative writing talents. Unscrupulous business partners, lying accountants or national recession are preferred to your tendency to buy high and sell low.

I see no shame in filing bankruptcy as long as the reason is civilized. A list of former bankrupts in your community may convince you that, within this club, one meets a better class of people.

LENDING STANDARDS

Lending standards vary according to the policies of the lender. However, the following is typical.

Your loan application must be in writing and signed by all applicants. The lender receives a credit report on the basis of the information contained on your application. A record of any one of the following may result in denial of a loan:

1. Slow payment records.
2. Previous mortgage loan defaults or foreclosures.
3. Previous credit written off as bad debts.
4. Late charges assessed.
5. Bankruptcies.
6. Repossessions.
7. Liens.
8. Wage garnishments.
9. Outstanding judgments.

Interest Rate	20 Years	25 Years	29 Years	30 Years
8.75	8.84	8.22	7.93	7.87
9	9.00	8.39	8.11	8.05
9.25	9.16	8.56	8.29	8.23
9.5	9.32	8.74	8.47	8.41
9.75	9.49	8.91	8.65	8.59
10	9.75	9.09	8.83	8.78
10.25	9.82	9.27	9.01	8.97
10.5	9.99	9.45	9.20	9.15
10.75	10.16	9.63	9.38	9.34
11	10.33	9.81	9.57	9.53
11.25	10.49	9.98	9.75	9.72
11.5	10.66	10.16	9.94	9.91
11.75	10.84	10.35	10.13	10.10
12	11.01	10.53	10.32	10.29
12.25	11.19	10.72	10.52	10.48
12.5	11.36	10.90	10.71	10.67
12.75	11.54	11.09	10.90	10.87
13	11.72	11.28	11.09	11.06
13.25	11.89	11.48	11.29	11.26
13.5	12.07	11.66	11.48	11.45
13.75	12.25	11.85	11.68	11.65
14	12.44	12.04	11.88	11.85
14.25	12.62	12.23	12.07	12.05
14.5	12.80	12.42	12.27	12.25
14.75	12.98	12.61	12.47	12.44

10. Frequent changes of employment without compensating salary increases.

Since most applicants have at least one past indiscretion, the lender will either overlook it or ask you to explain. In reviewing your credit report, lenders consider your recent credit pattern of more significance than past difficulties.

Two ratios are used by the loan officer in determining eligibility:

1. Total housing expense (principal, interest, taxes and insurance) cannot exceed 25 percent of *gross* monthly income.

and

2. Total housing expense plus total monthly long term (10 months or more) debt cannot exceed one third of gross monthly income.

This means that a buyer with a $1,600 per month gross income and no other debt can afford a monthly payment of up to $400. However, the same buyer with a $200 car payment (with more than 10 months remaining) could not afford the home. This second buyer could only afford approximately a $335 monthly payment.

By using the table on page 41 and by matching the interest rate with the term of the loan, you are able to find the cost per month (in dollars) of principal and interest per $1,000 of a mortgage.

EXAMPLE:

Sale price of building	$70,000.00
Minus down payment (20 percent)	14,000.00
Equals mortgage	56,000.00
Annual taxes	800.00
Annual homeowner's insurance premium	200.00
Interest rate	9.75
Length of loan (term)	30 years

Then:

Principal and interest = 56 × 8.59	481.04
Taxes = 800/12 =	66.67
Insurance = 220/12	18.33
Total monthly payment = (principal, interest, taxes and insurance)	$ 566.04

REAL ESTATE/OTHER INVESTMENTS/INFLATION

The following table will help clarify real estate's investment performance over the last 10 years as compared to alternative investments.

Triple A bonds	7.7%
Municipal bonds (tax-free)	5.8%
Common stock appreciation	2–3%
Savings accounts	4.7%
Real estate appreciation	10.1%

Again, keep in mind that real estate is commonly leveraged at 5:1. This makes the actual return to the investor 50 percent per year! This figure does not include closing costs incurred in both buying and selling, but you get the point.

OTHER MORTGAGE CONSIDERATIONS

Most people are more at home having a tooth extracted than reading a first mortgage; however, the theory is rather simple. The buyer signs two instruments, a judgment note and a mortgage document. The note is the buyer's agreement to repay his debt to the bank in definite installments with interest over a fixed period of years. The mortgage document spells out not only the rights of the bank, but the obligations of the buyer. These include not only the prompt payment of your debt in accordance with the note, but payment of all real estate taxes and assessments and maintenance of adequate fire insurance. The mortgage document also requires the buyer to keep his property in a good state of repair and to seek authorization from the bank before making any major improvements to the property. This last obligation seems curious as you would think the bank could only rejoice in any addition to its investment. The problem is the owner's good sense. A Byzantine cupola erected on the roof of a bi-level does not enhance the bank's investment.

All mortgages also contain an acceleration clause. An invoking of this clause is the first step in foreclosure. Should the buyer be delinquent in his payments, and despite the fact that the mortgage note carries a 29-year term, the bank may declare the entire debt due immediately.

In some states, many mortgages have prepayment penalties. These cash penalties are deferred until the buyer sells his property, at which time he may be required to pay the bank four or five thousand dollars in the form of penalties. Problems can be avoided in this area by asking the banker upon applying for a loan whether this policy exists. You are well advised to stay away from this type of mortgage.

The maximum rate of interest which may be charged on mortgages secured by real estate usually is limited by state law. To charge interest in excess of this rate is called usury. Closely related to the state usury laws is the Federal Truth in Lending Regulations. These regulations require the lender to fully disclose all the costs of the loan including interest and all service and loan charges.

PREDICTING FUTURE INTEREST RATES

In the long run (two years or more), interest rates will be higher; 15–18 percent is not unthinkable. However, in the short run (one year or less) interest rates will do one of three things: (a) rise, (b) fall or (c) stay the same. This is another way of saying that mortgage loan rates are solely a function of government economic policy and this policy is unpredictable in the short run, but quite predictable in the long term—ludicrous.

CHAPTER 4

CREATIVE FINANCING

*The charges [against Bert Lance]
were greatly exaggerated. . . .
Bert [Lance], I'm proud of you.*

Remarks by Jimmy Carter
upon the forced resignation of
the director of the Office
of Management and Budget.

*More than eight hundred
young brokers and bankers
burst into prolonged applause*

Time, Oct. 10, 1977

*C*reative financing is trade talk for financing buyers who don't have the money necessary for a down payment or who have inordinately high debt-to-income ratios. In most cases, these problems can be easily overcome. The only serious obstacle in satisfying the investor's "edifice complex" is unemployment. In addition, the reader will be comforted in knowing all of the methods discussed have at least one foot inside that safe zone called legality.

THE REASON FOR INTEREST

A lender's moral right to collect interest on money rests principally on his entitlement to a reward for risk taking. Currently, only about 1 percent of all home mortgages end in default. Of these, the lender rarely loses anything since the equity in the home is high enough not only to ensure the bank's return but to cover any expenses of foreclosure. In other words, given the present underwriting standards the middle class must conform to, lenders take no risk. Of course, a fast-talking swashbuckler with a telephone in his car can always get a business loan with little or no trouble. It is with these loans, generally large, that our banks unwittingly take risks and never on a home mortgage.

It is the function of creative financing to restore to lenders their ancient and glorious role of risk bearers to the nonrich. Furthermore, it restores noble purpose to their lives.

ALL THE THINGS
BERT LANCE KNOWS BUT AIN'T TELLIN'

The "pledge" is a financing device well known to all the old-timers in the real estate business. Unfortunately, in the last ten years this method is very rarely employed. I suspect the increasing willingness of mom and pop to come up with the down payment (get the kids off to a good start and all that) has reduced the pledge to secondary importance. Another reason for the demise of the pledge is that most real estate salesmen are unfamiliar with the concept or, if they are, don't mention it once mom and pop have made their commitment. Any attempt to improve things at this stage may result in the salesman "improving" himself out of a sales commission. Here's how it works.

The seller, mom and pop, or any third party, deposits in the buyer's lending institution all or part of the down payment. This account is then frozen. The third party (pledgee) not only gets the toaster but may withdraw the interest and that portion of the principal being reduced by the buyer's monthly payment. Of course, if the buyer misses a monthly payment, it is made up from the pledgee's account. The advantages to this type of financing are: (a) these loans are easy to arrange and (b) the bank pays the interest on the down-payment loan.

Stocks or bonds may also be pledged as security for a loan; however, the lender may allow you only 60 to 85 percent (depending on the stock) of the stock's current market value. The stockholder, of course, continues to receive dividends while his stock is being held by the bank.

Here is an interesting variation of the pledge. Let's assume the buyer wants to purchase an $80,000 house and has the 20 percent down payment ($16,000). The buyer may "give" this money to a third party (not without a written agreement between the two).

1. The pledgee then deposits this money in the pledge account. The advantage to the buyer is considerable. He gets interest on his down payment. This interest amounts to $1,320, which is more than enough to cover his property taxes. In three to five years, the buyer may ask for his pledge account to be released. The lender will have little or no objection to this as the home has appreciated to such an extent that the buyer would have at least 50 percent equity at this time. This financing method has the effect, in time, of a no-money-down loan; and the down payment, when retrieved after five years with interest compounded, is $23,783 on a $16,000 investment.

2. Using the salesman's commission as all or part of the down payment is a financing method many buyers either don't think of or don't have the stomach for. This is how it's done. Select a

salesman with a solid sales record. He is more apt not to need the money immediately. Ask him at the beginning if he's willing to lend his commission on the transaction. On a $50,000 transaction, the salesman's commission will vary from $625 to $5,000. Once he's satisfied that the transaction can't be completed without the loan of his commission, he can only resort to the third law of real estate: "It's better to have it owed to you than get screwed out of it."

He'll have you sign a judgment note for his commission—possibly for three years—with 36 equal installments and, just to make sure you adhere to the Divine Law, will record the note as a lien on your property. In case you renege on your monthly commitment to him, he is able to collect in full (plus accrued interest) on the future sale of your home. You may choose to deal directly with the owner of the real estate company as his share of the commission is greater than any of his salesmen. He not only is entitled to the sales commission (a percentage of the total) but also, as owner, the company share.

3. Becoming a real estate salesman may be the best method of all for the investor to follow, as a) most firms do not consider full-time participation necessary; b) inside information is more readily available; c) the salesman is the first to know when a "hot" property becomes available and d) you receive a commission on all properties you buy and sell for your own account (this will range from 2 to 10 percent of the transaction).

Licensing requirements are controlled by the individual states. Check with your local realtor for particulars. However, as a general rule, becoming licensed is somewhat more difficult than getting a social security card, but considerably easier than getting into the army.

I honestly believe that in the future everyone will be a licensed real estate salesman for the simple reason that no one can afford not to be. The average homeowner buys and sells 4.5 homes during his lifetime. Assuming a $60,000 median sales price, this adds up to something like $10,000 in commissions.

4. Borrowing from family is quite easy as long as you keep it

below $100. Any amount in excess of that, say $5,000, puts a real strain on the typical family tree. It isn't that your family wants to keep you in economic bondage; it's just that they don't want to be reduced to eating bark. Therefore it's a good idea when seeking a family loan to use the same procedure and comportment you would use when applying at a bank. A written financial statement is not out of order and can only increase your chances of success.

Being turned down for a loan by a bank is one thing, but being refused by a member of the family frequently results in a bitterness that lasts beyond the grave.

The first-home buyers are typically a newly married couple with no children (empty nesters). Since both husband and wife work, they have a high family income ($25,000–$35,000) and no money. The expenses incurred in setting up a household are high enough to burn through any savings account. A common method used in financing these buyers is for them to arrange for a family loan for the down payment, usually from mom and pop. It's a good idea for the buyers to lay a little "respectability" on this "family affair" by signing a promissory note (with interest). It helps the memory to say nothing of the ego. As for borrowing money from a friend, decide which you need most. There is no real need for the buyer to inform the bank of the source of the down payment. If, however, the lender insists for record purposes on knowing the origin of this money, the buyer may have his "angel" submit an instrument called a gift letter. This letter simply states that the buyer's down payment is a gift and repayment is not expected.

5. Properties that the trade calls "handyman specials" are frequently unmortgageable. They are not, however, unfinanceable. It is also important to clarify what is meant by a "handyman special." This is not a building that wants for a little "touch up" here and there. It's rather the type of building that one enters and is immediately overcome by a concern for his/her own well-being. In many cases serious structural problems are present. Lenders consider this type of loan too risky as they are not only gambling on the buyer's ability to repay but his ability to perform satisfactory repairs. In addition, the bank is also gambling that the build-

ing won't be condemned or, for that matter, that it will still be erect after five years.

This type of building can best be financed with a promissory note. This is a short-term loan, usually 6 months to two years, with an interest rate 2–3 percent above the conventional loan market. With this type of loan, there are no monthly payments to worry about as the entire loan (principal and interest) is repaid upon the due date of the note. Before this date arrives, the buyer has the option of either getting a 30-year mortgage loan on his restored building or selling it.

6. Your own home may be the best source of freeing up investment capital. There are two ways this can be done, and one may be right for you.

(a) *Refinancing.* This method, briefly stated, consists of selling your home to yourself and keeping some of the equity.

For example, six years ago you bought a home for $40,000 with 20 percent down. During this period, two things happened: (1) your original mortgage balance of $32,000 has decreased to about $29,500 and (2) your home has appreciated to, let's say, $72,000. You now have $42,500 in equity, and since lenders will lend 80 percent of the fair market value of your home minus the current mortgage balance, then you may free up as much as $28,100.

$$\$72,000 \times 80\% - \$29,500 = \$28,100$$

You must pay the closing costs on this transaction and, assuming these add up to $1,100, you then have $27,000 of investable funds which can then be used to buy more property or substantially improve your own home.

This is the good news. The bad news is that your old loan terms were probably 7.5 percent (remember that) on a $32,000 original balance with 24 years remaining. Your new terms are, say, 10 percent on a $57,600 balance for 30 years. Your new monthly principal and interest is $505.73 versus $224.00. This $281.73 increase in your monthly payment may, for you, be unendurable. If so, then you may consider a:

(b) *Second Mortgage.* All but sixteen states allow a homeowner to take out a second mortgage. These same states are probably those that don't allow you to keep your Pillsbury Bake-off winnings.

The interest rate on a second mortgage (currently about 15 percent) is higher and the period of the loan is shorter (generally a maximum of 10 years); however, once you pay off this second mortgage, your monthly principal and interest payment reverts back to $224.00. The monthly cost of a $25,000 second mortgage at 15 percent for 10 years is $403.33. Therefore, your total monthly payment on both the first and second mortgage would be $627.33.

Both refinancing and obtaining a second mortgage have now become a routine way of borrowing. Due to the recent, rapid appreciation of housing, lenders no longer show hesitancy in granting a second mortgage. If your income can support the new (higher) monthly payment, you'll get the loan. However, the investor must weigh the increase in his monthly payment against the return on his newly found investable funds.

Let us suppose your home has appreciated to an appraised value of $65,000 and your original 7.5 percent $30,000 loan has been reduced to a current balance of $27,000. Since you may refinance 80 percent of the current value of your home, or $52,000, you then may free up $25,000 of investable funds ($52,000–$27,000). Since your bank will insist on a 25 percent down payment on any investment property you buy (i.e., apartment building), you are then qualified to buy a $100,000 building. Of course, your monthly principal and interest payment has increased by $237.20 per month ($2,846.40 per year) and you must pay the closing costs on the new loan; however, you are now receiving all the economic advantages of controlling an additional $100,000 in real estate. If appreciation were the only economic advantage to owning real estate—it's not—and if in your area real estate is appreciating at 10 percent per year, then a $10,000 increase in your net worth is realizable in your first year of ownership. This alone is more than enough to compensate the "player" for any increase in his monthly payment.

There are many other solid reasons for refinancing your home such as debt consolidation, college education or starting a business venture. It may make more sense to you to borrow at 10 percent for 30 years instead of 12 to 18 percent for four years, as is common on installment loans.

7. Let us assume that both the buyer and seller agree on a sale price of $50,000 for a particular piece of property. Let us also assume that the buyer's income is more than enough to support the monthly payment but that he does not have the down payment necessary ($10,000). The buyer may then submit a contract for $40,000 along with a promissory note for $10,000 at 9 percent and due in five years. The seller protects his investment by immediately recording the note as a lien on the property.

If, however, the seller needs all of the equity out of his house in order to finance his next, then he may accept a promissory note for, say, $10,800 and discount the note (sell it to a bank or finance company for less than its face value) for $10,000. The buyer in effect has a no-money-down loan and the seller sold his home and either 1) immediately retrieved all of his equity or 2) has a secure (backed by real estate) five-year investment yielding him 9 percent.

8. When a buyer purchases property by using a VA or FHA loan he is asking the seller to discount his property. This discount varies from 1 percent to 9 percent of the buyer's mortgage, depending on the current money market. Many sellers are unwilling to sell if they are required to pay, say, a $1,500 "penalty." This problem can be overcome by having the buyer pay to the seller at closing $1,500 for the gas range, which, in any case, was staying with the property. This amounts to a personal property transaction and is covered by a written bill of sale. The seller is thus mollified by being reimbursed for his extra selling expense.

9. On occasion, a buyer may not have quite enough for a 20 percent down payment. He may have only $10,000 to put down on a building requiring $12,000 as a down payment. In this instance, the seller may consider increasing the sale price of his home by $2,000 and then rebating this money back to the buyer

at closing. Both buyer and seller are advised not to carry this trick too far, as the lender must appraise the property and too much "phantom" money will only result in a low appraisal and, therefore, no loan.

10. Non-buying real estate. The premise of this book is the rapid accumulation of wealth through the purchase of small and medium-size real estate investments. However, currently, and in many markets, enormous short-term profits can be realized by buying but not taking delivery on new construction. This type of investing is the soul of commodity market investment and has its stock market equivalent in the options exchange. Since actual ownership never takes place, this is not real estate, but pure financing.

This investment method consists of the "player" selecting a new and preferably large subdivision and buying for future delivery the model of his choice. Since most subdivisions are built in sections giving various delivery dates, the buyer is advised to select a home in the last section to be built, thus ensuring the latest possible closing date. In order for this method to make sense to the investor the delivery date may be as short as six months and as long as eighteen months into the future. In a strong local market and with a well-planned and designed subdivision, any model within that subdivision will appreciate from 10 to 50 percent per year. The reason for this tremendous increase is not only the usual reason of inflation but the builder's tendency to price his product artificially low at the beginning in order to build sales momentum and get his project off to a good start.

In order to make this ploy work, the buyer should be a current homeowner and employ the following fiction:

BUYER: My wife and I have decided to buy your three-bedroom ranch which I believe you call your "Stratford-on-Avon." (The only universal constant in real estate is the builder's obsession with English names. Can you imagine a builder referring to his models as the "The Budapest," "The Saigon," "The Calcutta" or "The Warsaw"?)

SALESMAN: Would you like to include any of our options?

BUYER: Yes, we would like a fireplace, patio, ceramic foyer and would also like to upgrade the carpeting to "Kitschalon."

SALESMAN: The total cost of your home with your options and ready for occupancy this time next year is $74,995. In order to buy this home, you'll have to sign this contract and give us a check for 10 percent of the purchase price ($7,500).

BUYER: We're perfectly willing to sign the contract, however, my wife and I don'thave anything near $7,500 in savings. We do, however, have $25,000 equity in our present house and only upon its sale can we give you this deposit. Since we're willing buyers, there must be another way you can "work this out."

SALESMAN: Yes there is. We will accept a check for $500 and you'll have to sign a promissory note for the balance ($7,000) and due upon the closing of your home. Your interest in the note will be 10 percent.

Both parties to this "ballet" are happy. The buyers are happy because they are guaranteed delivery of a home a year hence and at a fixed price of $74,995. Their total cash investment is only $500.

The builder is happy since he not only sold a home but has $500 and a promissory note which he immediately discounts to a commercial bank (sells it to a bank for less than its face value, say, $6,300). This total of $6,800 is then used as working capital.

The buyer's next step is to go home and begin taking all the necessary steps in making a baby since nothing is required of him regarding this transaction for the next nine months. At this time —three months before closing of his new home—he then offers this home for sale. The price of the "Stratford-on-Avon" is now, say, $89,995 and if he prices his model at $88,500 a quick sale is certain. This gross profit of $14,000 is a quite plausible, even modest, prediction. It is important to know that it is quite legal to sell a home that you do not have title to and attorneys refer to this procedure as "selling equitable title." To put it another way, you are not selling a home but rather the *right* to buy a particular home at a fixed price. There is no risk involved in this "game" since the worst that can happen is you'll have to sell your present home and actually buy your new construction. It is therefore a good idea to make sure that the model you pick out is one you can afford and be comfortable living in.

A good friend of mine made $174,000 last year by using this device. He did this by having contracts outstanding on eight homes in eight different subdivisions simultaneously. I do not recommend this to the novice due to the higher risk involved. This is a very fast track and of course you have to be prepared to speak a number of inoperative statements (lies) to both builders and bankers. However, anyone who once did this declares it to be far superior to working.

11. Tapping your life insurance policy for investment capital. The typical life insurance policy satisfies two needs: protection and savings. While everyone understands the protection benefits—your beneficiaries are paid the face value of the policy in the event you go to room temperature—few people are fully aware of the savings function. Here is how it works.

Suppose at age of 30 years you take out a $20,000 ordinary life policy. Assuming an average state of health, your premium would be approximately $400 per year. This premium would yield a guaranteed interest rate plus a dividend which may give you a total of 5 percent per year. While this yield rate is not exactly heroic, keep in mind it's tax free and therefore may be more than you realize. After twelve years, your policy has a cash value, including dividends, of approximately $5,000. You may borrow this money by signing a cash value loan agreement and in so doing the following things happen:

(a) Your protection is reduced from $20,000 to $15,000.

(b) Your loan of $5,000 is considered a prepaid benefit and in the event you die while this loan is outstanding the remainder of your loan balance is considered to be paid in full.

(c) Your interest rate on this loan (depending on the terms of your policy) will range from 5 percent to 8 percent. These are the lowest interest rates available.

(d) Your loan repayment is not tied to any fixed schedule. You may repay this loan at your own convenience and in accordance with your own budget. You may even decide never to repay the loan.

(e) In order to keep your policy in effect, you must of course continue to pay your $400 per year premium; however, at this stage in the life of your policy, you will be getting a yearly dividend of approximately $200.

(f) The wise investor may decide to use part of this policy dividend to purchase term insurance sufficient to cover his cash-value loan, thereby restoring his full policy benefit of $20,000. At 42, this would amount to only about $35 per year. This method of "discovering" a down payment is a favorite of mine as it allows your life insurance to do triple duty: protection, real estate investment and savings.

12. In many cases, buyers do not qualify for a loan not because their incomes are too low but rather their long-term debt is too high. Long-term debt is generally considered to be any obligation in excess of ten months. Car payments are the most common long-term debts. Should a buyer's car payment be $175 per month and should this factor alone preclude the buyer from getting a loan, he may then sign over the car title to his father but, of course, continue to make the payments. The buyer has erased a long-term debt from his financial statement.

13. I know of a small, modestly successful businessman who wanted to expand his operation. After being turned down for a business loan at three banks, he hit upon the idea of borrowing $50,000 in cash from his wealthy brother-in-law. He then stuffed this money in the vault of a local bank and waited some weeks before applying for a loan. His discussion with the loan officer wasn't going well until, as an afterthought, he ushered the loan officer into the vault. Upon displaying his box, choking with $100 bills, and after a number of knowing smiles and winks were exchanged, he got his loan. He then dutifully returned the money to his brother-in-law.

This businessman didn't know too much about financing but he knew a great deal about human nature (a more enduring talent).

He correctly guessed that a banker would be beguiled by what was apparently tax fraud.

14. Having a loan co-signed. Many times a buyer's debt-to-income ratio may be a little short of what the lender considers ideal. In this case the buyer may find a co-signer, in most cases, the buyer's parents. This type of financing is easy to arrange and does not require any cash from the co-signer. It does require the co-signer to sign the mortgage document and note, thereby making the co-signer responsible for the monthly payment should the buyer fall behind.

15. Builder's credit. Here's an interesting way of buying new construction with little or no money down. It can be done only with new construction and only with the connivance of the builder.

Buy a home from a builder and order all of his options such as a fireplace, air conditioner, upgraded carpeting, sodded lawn, etc. After your loan is approved by the bank but before these options are installed, cancel them and accept a builder's credit for their value. You can easily load $12,000 in options on an $80,000 home, and this serves to reduce what would normally be a $16,000 down payment to only $4,000. This trick may be difficult to pull off during "good times" for the builder but it is quite feasible during his down cycles.

16. Here's one for the seller. Should you be unable to sell your home at the listed price of $52,000, instead of reducing your price to $50,000, try offering a $2,000 carpeting allowance to the buyer. This has the same effect of reducing the price by $2,000 and makes no difference in the proceeds you realize from the sale. It does, however, make a big difference to the buyer. He now receives an extra $2,000 at closing under the fiction that he will use it to replace your "worn" carpeting. By doing this, the seller a) helps the buyer's down-payment problem or b) since real estate is commonly mortgaged it allows a buyer to buy a $10,000 better home. The advantage to the seller is that he expands the market for his home which results in a quicker sale.

17. Wrap-around mortgage. This underused type of financing is

of principal benefit to the seller. This financing method consists in the buyer agreeing to pay to the seller (in one mortgage) the balance of the seller's original mortgage at current interest rates plus another indebtedness which is the difference between the sales price minus the down payment, if any, minus the original loan balance.

EXAMPLE:

Sale price	$150,000
Buyer's down payment	− 25,000
Buyer's wrap-around mortgage balance and terms	$125,000 @ 10% for 20 years

Seller's original loan balance and terms $65,000 @ 7 percent for 20 years.

Every month, the buyer sends the seller a check reflecting a mortgage of $125,000 at 10 percent for 20 years. However, the seller's original loan, taken in 1971, was only 7 percent. This 3.5 percent spread on $65,000 is additional interest income to the seller above his regular interest collection.

The buyer may also benefit from the seller holding this type of mortgage in that the buyer may avoid paying points and he may be able to buy property with a lower down payment than a bank would demand.

18. Land lease. The land lease is an established home ownership concept in Europe and is frequently used for commercial, office and apartment buildings in the United States. The land lease has application wherever land costs are high.

Due to the historic low cost of land in the United States, this type of ownership has yet to become important in the American residential market. However, I believe rising land and building costs will make the land lease a standard ownership form of the future.

With a land lease, a builder sells a home but retains ownership of the land. The land is then rented to the buyer from 50 to 99 years at, say, $50 to $100 a month. This not only significantly reduces the cost of housing but since banks can give the buyer credit for the land in making his down payment, the down payment is drastically reduced. For example a $60,000 home built on a $12,000 lot would give a total sales price of $72,000 and, with 20 percent down, a $14,400 down payment. However, since the bank credits the buyer with the land cost ($12,000), his actual down payment is only $2,400.

Although a 99-year lease has the effect of ownership (the banks think so), I can foresee, at least initially, a certain psychological barrier on the part of the buyer. However, rising costs will adjust this.

SUMMARY

Being broke is a sorry excuse for not buying a home or any other real estate investment. It is never an excuse to continue renting. The overwhelming economic advantages to ownership (appreciation, principle repayment, and tax write-offs) make renting too expensive for the average wage earner to consider.

Since lenders are quite willing to lend to the rich, it is your job to appear so, and creative financing is your method. If you find this disturbing, you may take comfort from Proverbs XXVIII, 20: "He that maketh haste to be rich shall not be innocent."

As a home buyer or investor, your objective is to buy the most home at the lowest price with the least amount of down payment and consistent with your ability to meet the monthly payment. While stretching yourself to afford real estate makes sound economic sense, burying yourself with an unreasonable monthly payment does not. You are the best judge of the maximum payment you can afford, and, keep in mind, going through foreclosure proceedings does nothing for your self-esteem.

CHAPTER 5

_T_AXES

_A poor man's roast
and a rich man's death
are smelled far away._

—Anonymous

*A*ll successful people know that paying taxes is stupid. They also know that going to the penitentiary is even stupider. Fortunately, a happy medium is obtainable by exploiting certain provisions in the tax code. These are called shelters or, if you are not currently taking advantage of them, they are called loopholes. This concept, which is sometimes explained as tax avoidance, is a right, but tax evasion is a crime. This should not overload anyone's sophistry. The successful also know that the tax laws favor the self-employed and investor and not the wage earner or salaried employee. And finally, they have a clearer understanding that in an age of confiscatory taxation, yearly income is less important than yearly after-tax income, or precisely, the annual increase in one's estate.

THE PROGRESSIVE INCOME TAX

Our income tax is progressive. Higher incomes are subject to a higher percentage of tax. However, it is important to know just who is getting "progressed." The tax tables are deceptive on this point. No one is taxed more than 50 percent of his earned income. Even with investment (unearned) income, avoiding paying taxes in excess of 50 percent is possible with enlightened tax planning.

The "progressed" are those people commonly referred to as the middle class. The incremental rate (tax bracket) increases from 14 to 62 percent (filing singly) in the first $50,000 of income; during the next $50,000 of income it rises by only 8 percent.

YOUR TAX BRACKET

Few people know their bracket, and for those that don't, they always underestimate it. If you earn $26,000 and pay $5,200 in federal tax, it means that only 20 percent of your earnings are devoted to paying income tax. Your tax bracket, if you are single, is 45 percent. Since a progressive tax requires you to pay more dollars on the last few thousand you earn than on the first few thousand, the average tax you pay is 20 percent, but the tax rate on the last $1,000 is 45 percent. It is the percentage of tax paid on the last $1,000 of earnings (your tax bracket) that is important in making all investment and financial decisions.

And yet the tax tables are again deceptive in that they fail to include state income tax or social security. All but six states have an income tax and this varies from 2 to 10 percent. In addition, you can add 6 percent for social security (8 percent if you're self-employed). In the most extreme example, this puts the single, self-employed, New Yorker with a taxable income of $26,000 in the 63 percent tax bracket! I do not include fuel, sales and property taxes, nor do I include the "bad habits" taxes on alcohol, cigarettes or playing cards. These have nothing to do with your tax bracket. They are penalties for use and have nothing to do with your income. In any event, 63 percent is enough.

If we assume a taxpayer is in the 50 percent tax bracket, and as the tables on pages 64 and 65 show, this is easier than you may think, then any $1,000 increase in earnings results in only $500 kept after tax. Likewise, any $1,000 deduction results in only a $500 cost after tax.

THE TAX SHELTER

Our tax code and its infinite exceptions, interpretations, litigations, loopholes and attempts to close loopholes is unbelievably complex. This complexity is a result of legislative efforts to implement domestic policy. For example, tax credits for upgrading home insulation help implement a natural energy conservation policy.

Tax shelters are a means of using our tax laws to lessen and/or defer tax liability. However, in recent years, the words "tax shelter," like neo-colonialism, have inherited a bad connotation. This is not without good reason. Except for real estate, most tax shelters that are not swindles lose more money than they save in taxes and you can't make money by losing money. These tax shelters are always exotic (cattle breeding, walnut groves, sports teams, etc.) and I suspect that this is their prin-

TAX RATE TABLE FOR UNMARRIED INDIVIDUALS

| Taxable Income | | Income Tax Liability | | |
Over—	But less than—	Tax Bracket		
$ 0	$ 500	14%	$ 0 plus	of income over $ 0
$ 500	$ 1,000	15%	$ 70 plus	of income over $ 500
$ 1,000	$ 1,500	16%	$ 145 plus	of income over $ 1,000
$ 1,500	$ 2,000	17%	$ 225 plus	of income over $ 1,500
$ 2,000	$ 4,000	19%	$ 310 plus	of income over $ 2,000
$ 4,000	$ 6,000	21%	$ 690 plus	of income over $ 4,000
$ 6,000	$ 8,000	24%	$ 1,110 plus	of income over $ 6,000
$ 8,000	$ 10,000	25%	$ 1,590 plus	of income over $ 8,000
$ 10,000	$ 12,000	27%	$ 2,090 plus	of income over $ 10,000
$ 12,000	$ 14,000	29%	$ 2,630 plus	of income over $ 12,000
$ 14,000	$ 16,000	31%	$ 3,210 plus	of income over $ 14,000
$ 16,000	$ 18,000	34%	$ 3,830 plus	of income over $ 16,000
$ 18,000	$ 20,000	36%	$ 4,510 plus	of income over $ 18,000
$ 20,000	$ 22,000	38%	$ 5,230 plus	of income over $ 20,000
$ 22,000	$ 26,000	40%	$ 5,990 plus	of income over $ 22,000
$ 26,000	$ 32,000	45%	$ 7,590 plus	of income over $ 26,000
$ 32,000	$ 38,000	50%	$ 10,290 plus	of income over $ 32,000
$ 38,000	$ 44,000	55%	$ 13,290 plus	of income over $ 38,000
$ 44,000	$ 50,000	60%	$ 16,590 plus	of income over $ 44,000
$ 50,000	$ 60,000	62%	$ 20,190 plus	of income over $ 50,000
$ 60,000	$ 70,000	64%	$ 26,390 plus	of income over $ 60,000
$ 70,000	$ 80,000	66%	$ 32,790 plus	of income over $ 70,000
$ 80,000	$ 90,000	68%	$ 39,390 plus	of income over $ 80,000
$ 90,000	$100,000	69%	$ 46,190 plus	of income over $ 90,000
$100,000		70%	$ 53,090 plus	of income over $100,000

TAX RATE TABLE FOR MARRIED INDIVIDUALS FILING JOINT RETURNS AND FOR SURVIVING SPOUSES

Taxable Income		Income Tax Liability		
Over—	But less than—		Tax Bracket	
$ 0	$ 1,000	$ plus	14%	of income over $ 0
$ 1,000	$ 2,000	$ 140 plus	15%	of income over $ 1,000
$ 2,000	$ 3,000	$ 290 plus	16%	of income over $ 2,000
$ 3,000	$ 4,000	$ 450 plus	17%	of income over $ 3,000
$ 4,000	$ 8,000	$ 620 plus	19%	of income over $ 4,000
$ 8,000	$ 12,000	$ 1,380 plus	22%	of income over $ 8,000
$ 12,000	$ 16,000	$ 2,260 plus	25%	of income over $ 12,000
$ 16,000	$ 20,000	$ 3,260 plus	28%	of income over $ 16,000
$ 20,000	$ 24,000	$ 4,380 plus	32%	of income over $ 20,000
$ 24,000	$ 28,000	$ 5,660 plus	36%	of income over $ 24,000
$ 28,000	$ 32,000	$ 7,100 plus	39%	of income over $ 28,000
$ 32,000	$ 36,000	$ 8,660 plus	42%	of income over $ 32,000
$ 36,000	$ 40,000	$10,340 plus	45%	of income over $ 36,000
$ 40,000	$ 44,000	$12,140 plus	48%	of income over $ 40,000
$ 44,000	$ 52,000	$14,060 plus	50%	of income over $ 44,000
$ 52,000	$ 64,000	$18,060 plus	53%	of income over $ 52,000
$ 64,000	$ 76,000	$24,420 plus	55%	of income over $ 64,000
$ 76,000	$ 88,000	$31,020 plus	58%	of income over $ 76,000
$ 88,000	$100,000	$37,980 plus	60%	of income over $ 88,000
$100,000	$120,000	$45,180 plus	62%	of income over $100,000
$120,000	$140,000	$57,580 plus	64%	of income over $120,000
$140,000	$160,000	$70,380 plus	66%	of income over $140,000
$160,000	$180,000	$83,580 plus	68%	of income over $160,000

cipal allure. The "investors" know little or nothing about the venture and because of this, disaster soon follows. If there ever was a favorable tax loophole to these shelters, recent tax law changes have closed it. A better alternative to investing $10,-000 in the typical tax shelter is to invest $10,000 in lottery tickets. You are losing 50 percent of your investment but—who knows—you may win the million.

Real estate is the *only* legitimate tax-shelter game in town, and due to widely held ownership (votes) our tax laws will continue to make it so.

TAX CONSIDERATIONS ON YOUR HOME

Certain expenses incurred in buying, occupying and selling your home have tax implications. It is important to know when each occurs. The exact date of the purchase or sale occurs on the day the deed is delivered. This is referred to as the closing or settlement date. That period in between is the period of occupation. On the day the sale or listing contract is signed or on the day possession is given, no taxable event occurs.

When a home is purchased, two things happen which are of tax consequence to the buyer:

1. He may deduct the lender's origination fee (points) from that year's taxes.
2. He is establishing a basis.

Points are considered prepaid interest and are used to reduce taxable income in the year the transaction took place. The basis is determined by including all costs incurred in acquiring and defending title. The following items constitute the basis.

(1) Purchase price	$50,000
(2) Title charges	120
(3) Survey	75
(4) Attorney's fee	150
(5) Revenue stamps	50
(6) Recording fee	21
Basis	$50,416

Items such as insurance, personal property or fuel-oil inventory are costs of ownership and do not affect the basis.

This basis, periodically adjusted, is, like a tattoo, something you will probably have for the rest of your life. Subsequent home expenditures which (a) increase the market value of the home (i.e., remodeling), (b) extend its useful life (i.e., restoration) or (c) convert it to an alternative use (i.e., modify the structure to commercial use) are upward adjustments to your basis. Likewise, certain events that reduce the value of your property, such as selling a portion of it, have a downward effect on your basis:

Original purchase price	$50,000
Plus costs involved in acquiring and defending title	+416
Equal original basis	$50,416
Add expenditures which have increased market value of property (family-room addition)	+12,000
Minus garage destroyed by fire	−2,500
Equal adjusted basis	$59,916

The adjusted basis ($59,916) is the figure used to compute the capital gain or loss on any subsequent sale or exchange of the property.

Capital improvements increase your adjusted basis but repairs don't. Moreover, since the property is for personal use, repairs are not a tax-deductible expense. Repairs are strictly a personal expense having no tax consequences.

Since it is in your interests to have the highest possible adjusted basis and since the distinction between repair and improvement is ambiguous, always give yourself the benefit of the doubt. Should you lose the argument during an audit, manfully deliver an honest and heartfelt apology and pay the nominal interest charge on the additional tax liability.

The only time repair costs have a tax effect is if they occur within 90 days prior to the sale of your home. These fix-up costs are considered necessary to enhance salability and are a downward adjustment on the sale price. Other downward adjustments to the sale price may include:

(1) Broker commissions
(2) Title insurance
(3) Attorney fees
(4) Revenue stamps
(5) VA or FHA discount points
(6) Survey

The difference between the adjusted sale price and the adjusted basis is the capital gain.

Assuming a $59,916 adjusted basis as in the above example, the owner, three years later, sells his home for $75,500. The broker's commission is 7 percent of the sale price. Title insurance, legal fees, revenue stamps and survey equal $421. Two months prior to the sale, the seller had his home painted in order to improve salability. This cost was $400.

Sale price	$75,500
Minus commission	−5,285
Minus other selling costs	−421
Minus fix-up expenses	−400
Equal adjusted sales price	$69,394
THEN	
Amount realized	$69,394
Minus adjusted basis	−59,916
Equal capital gain	$9,478

The capital gain of $9,478 is subject to a capital gains tax unless the seller purchases another home costing at least as much as the adjusted sales price of the old. He must buy his next home within one year prior to, or one year following, the sale of the old in order to qualify (if the buyer subsequently purchases new construction, the time allowed is extended to 18 months).

The basis of the buyer's new home is the purchase price, adjusted for closing costs, minus the capital gain of the old.

The above seller upgrades to a home costing $90,000. His closing costs are $1,800 and his unrecognized capital gain on his old home is $9,478.

THEN

Purchase price	$90,000
Minus closing costs	− 1,800
Equal adjusted purchase price	$88,200
Minus unrecognized capital gain	−9,478
Equal basis of new home	$78,722

Your basis is your baggage. You carry it with you throughout your real estate life. It is continually adjusted for subsequent purchases, sales, improvements or destructions. In your younger years, you are not avoiding the tax on capital gains but deferring it. After 30 years and four moves, a homeowner may easily accumulate an $80,000 capital gain. If so, the wisdom of deferring capital gain tax becomes clear. Recent legislation allows the homeowner, 55 years of age or older, a one-time exemption from capital gains tax on the first $100,000 of gain. This allows a 55-year-old homeowner to sell his home and rent or move to a less expensive single-family residence or condominium and enjoy, tax free, up to $100,000. And remember, if you are in the 50 percent tax bracket, $100,000 tax free equals $200,000 in earnings.

The length of time the property is owned is important in any consideration of capital gain. Property owned in excess of 12 months is considered "long term" capital gain and for less than 12 months "short term" capital gain. "Short term" capital gain is taxed at the same rate as ordinary income but "long term" gain has the effect of being taxed at one half the rate of ordinary income (the first 50 percent of gain is tax free).

If for some reason, you take your capital gain prior to age 55, you are taxed at only half the rate of ordinary income (earned income). The capital-gains game is like sex. When it is good, it is very, very good, but when it is bad, it is still pretty good.

If the purchase price of a new home is less than the adjusted sale price of the old, then some capital-gains tax must be paid.

A homeowner sells his old home at an adjusted sale price of

$69,394. His adjusted basis is $59,916. He buys another home costing $62,000.

Since the homeowner's new home cost less than the sale of his old, a capital gains liability is incurred. The difference between the adjusted cost of his new home ($62,000) and the adjusted sale price of his old home ($69,394) is $7,394. on this figure the typical homeowner must pay a 25 percent tax, or $1,848.50.

TAX CONSIDERATIONS DURING OWNERSHIP

As a homeowner, you are entitled to deduct from your gross income, during the current year, all mortgage interest payments and property taxes. On a $50,000, 10 percent, 30-year mortgage loan, a homeowner will pay approximately $4,992 in interest charges during the current year. Assuming his real estate taxes are $950, then his total deduction would be $5,948 for that year. If the homeowner is in the 45 percent bracket (and compared to a tenant in the same tax bracket), this represents to the homeowner an additional $2,676.60 in after-tax income.

LOWERING YOUR PROPERTY TAXES

Every real estate taxing authority has a procedure for property owners to follow in order to contest their taxes. Check with your local assessor for particulars.

It's not enough for the property owner to scream at the assessor, he must do more. He must justify. He must present a case, no matter how weak. He must allow the assessor or his delegate a high-minded way out of an aggravating situation. In some jurisdictions, the property owner may even offer a bribe, but before doing this he must make sure he knows the customs and procedures of the local market. This could be construed as a criminal offense rather than a quaint provincialism.

Levying property taxes is, at best, an imprecise art and you will never know if you are paying too much until you check. This is easier than you think since property taxes are a matter of public record. Should you check the tax rolls and find your property to be taxed higher than comparable properties in your area, you probably have a valid argument.

Should your taxes be in line with the rest of the area, you may still try for a break. This, of course, requires some salesmanship. An argument based on your neighbor having more than you and equal taxes is in order, (i.e., brick garage vs. frame, more square footage, etc.). Forget for a time any edges you may have over him.

However, if you find your taxes are too low, it's a good idea to allow the assessor to perform his municipal functions without the benefit of your nagging.

If you are turned down and still feel you have a valid argument, you may go through an appeal procedure beyond the assessor.

INHERITED PROPERTY

Most people, sooner or later, inherit property. When they do, they inherit the basis of the deceased. There are a few exceptions to this rule. The advice of an accountant should be sought in order to determine their benefit, if any.

HENRY GEORGE'S TAX POLICY

Henry George (1839–97) was a waiter, clerk, seaman, typesetter, gold prospector, newspaper publisher, writer, orator, economist, land reformer and perpetual losing candidate for political office. His only break with failure came with the publication of *Progress and Poverty* (1879). In it he popularizes and systemizes his "single tax" theory, the germ of which was, even then, a hundred years old.

His tax theories died with him, and yet I believe there is still something we can abstract from his writings.

If George were alive today, he would argue the unfairness of taxing vacant and fallow land at a rate considerably less than land used to give housing and employment to our citizens. The reverse should be true. Under current taxing policy, the home-owner and employer are taxed heavily while the speculator, whose estate increases as a result of the growth of the economy and not his individual effort, is nominally taxed.

To understand this concept is to understand the myth that the landlord or business (big or small) pay taxes. They don't. You do. These entities can treat their taxes only as a cost of doing business and pass this cost on to their customers. They are nothing more than tax-collection agencies for the government.

If taxes were to fall more equally on owners of improved and unimproved land, the following benefits can be expected to follow:

1. A reduction in land costs due to the elimination of the land speculator would result in a partial brake on the cost of housing.

2. A partial curb on the rising costs of goods and services due to a decrease in business operating expenses.

3. A reduction in the number of forced sales by homeowners due to ever-increasing taxes.

4. A tendency to employ all of our land to its highest and best use.

CREDITS FOR ENERGY SAVING DEVICES

You are entitled to a credit of 15 percent of the first $2,000 (maximum $300) you spend on labor and components to conserve energy in your own home. A tax credit is, of course, nobler than a deduction since a credit of $300 reduces your total tax bill by that amount. A deduction of $300 reduces only your taxable income by $300.

These energy conservation devices are limited to:

1. Insulation designed to reduce heat loss (or gain) of your home or water heater.

2. Storm or thermal doors and windows.

3. Caulking or weather stripping of doors or windows.

4. Clock thermostats or other automatic energy-saving set-back thermostats.

5. Furnace modifications designed to increase fuel efficiency, including replacement burners, modified flue openings and ignition systems that replace a gas pilot light.

6. Meters that display the cost of energy usuage.

You may also receive additional energy credit for amounts you spend on:

1. Solar-energy property (collectors, rockbeds, and heat exchangers) that transforms sunlight into heat or electricity.
2. Geothermal property which distributes the natural heat found in rocks or water.
3. Wind-energy property (windmills) which uses wind to produce energy (generally electricity) for residential purposes.

This credit is computed by taking 30 percent of the first $2,000 and 20 percent of the next $8,000 for a total maximum credit of $2,200.

PROPERTY-TAX CIRCUIT BREAKERS AND HOMESTEAD EXEMPTIONS

All fifty states have their own version of a property-tax relief program. They are primarily aimed at reducing the tax burden of the elderly. A circuit breaker goes into effect when your property-tax bill exceeds a set percentage of household income. The form of payment may be a direct reduction in the property-tax bill, a refundable credit against state income taxes or a cash refund.

Many states use another form of tax relief called a homestead exemption. This is typically available to all elderly owner-occupants and reduces property taxes by a specified dollar amount.

These programs are still somewhat of a secret, as 25 percent of those eligible are not taking advantage of them. The reason for this may be that this type of tax relief is not given automatically upon the individual reaching 65. You must apply for these programs at your county tax office.

Since this type of tax relief is state-administered, there are no universal rules covering eligibility or the amount and form of payment. Sixty-five, 62 and in one state (Kansas) 60 is the minimum age, while in others you may be qualified at any age. Homeowners in all but one state (North Dakota), homeowners and renters in others, or homeowners, renters and the disabled (at any age) are qualified. In those states that allow renters property-tax relief, it is assumed that a certain percentage of the rent, say 20 percent, is devoted to paying the landlord's tax bill.

The objective of these programs is to give tax relief to the elderly and to try to assure that no taxpayer pays an excessive portion of household income for property taxes.

CURRENT ALLOWABLE
MOVING-EXPENSE DEDUCTIONS

Whether you are changing employers, self-employed or transferred, and if your new job adds at least 35 miles commuting distance, you are eligible to deduct the following moving expenses:

1. *The costs of moving household goods.* This includes transporting, packing, in-transit storing and insuring. (Your automobile and family pet are included.)

2. *Travel expenses.* These include meals and lodging for yourself and your family while en route to your new residence.

3. *Pre-move househunting trips.* After obtaining work in your new location, you may deduct transportation, meals and lodging for you and your family while shopping for your new home.

4. *Expenses incurred in occupying temporary quarters.* Should you be unable to gain immediate occupancy in your new home, food and lodging are deductible in the interim. These expenses, along with pre-move house-hunting expenses, are limited to $1,-500.

Selling and buying expenses (commissions, attorney fees, etc.) are also deductible; however, the over-all moving-expense limitation is $3,000 and you will probably exceed this. Therefore, always claim the costs of pre-move househunting trips and temporary quarters (maximum $1,500) before you claim selling and buying expenses. The total in excess of $3,000 may then be used to (a) reduce the capital gain on the sale of your old home or to (b) increase the basis of your new home.

TAX CONSIDERATIONS ON INCOME PROPERTY

Losses fall in two categories: economic loss and accounting loss. An economic loss is a situation in which the cash outflow exceeds the cash inflow. While this type of loss is deductible, it certainly doesn't do anything for your economic well-being. An accounting loss is a loss "on paper" and does not necessarily reflect the facts. It is, however, this type of loss in which, in real estate, the investor and the IRS are most interested.

To understand the tax advantages of investment real estate or any tax shelter, it is first necessary to understand depreciation. Depreciation may be defined as the decrease in value of real property improvements (buildings) caused by deterioration or obsolescence. The IRS views the depreciation allowance as a means whereby the investor can recover his capital investment during the life of the investment. However, while the property is being depreciated on paper, due to inflation, it is, in fact, appreciating in market value. Therefore, the investor may consider depreciation as only a loss in value due to accounting procedure and something to be used as a deduction for income-tax purposes.

You cannot depreciate your own home but you can depreciate income property. In addition, only the building, not the land it sits on, may be depreciated. In fact, land does appreciate or depreciate according to the changes in desirability of the surrounding market, but for computing depreciation it is considered a constant.

The exact value of the land can be determined either by so stating on the sales contract or by employing the ratio used by your local tax assessor. However, 25 percent of the total purchase price is standard.

The IRS guideline for useful life on an apartment is 40 years and for a single-family dwelling 45 years. This is only a guideline and a shorter, more advantageous period can be justified given certain market or age conditions.

The nondepreciability of land, the estimated useful life of the building and the sale price determine the annual deduction for depreciation. The formula may be stated as follows:

Purchase Price — Land Value = Value of Building
Value of Building ÷ Useful Life = Annual depreciation deduction

A six-flat is bought for $120,000 of which 25 percent represents land value. It is a ten-year-old building to which the buyer assigns a 30-year useful life. If we use the straight-line method of depreciation:

THEN

$120,000 × 25% = $30,000 (land value)
$120,000 − 30,000 = $90,000 (building value)
$90,000 ÷ 30 (useful life) = $3,000 (annual deduction for depreciation)

The following practical economic consequences follow or are implied from the above example:

1. The typical net income on a building such as this in the first year of operation and after principal, interest, taxes, insurance and operating expenses are paid can be expected to be about $1,000.
2. Depreciation of $3,000 not only offsets the $1,000 income but the remaining $2,000 depreciation deduction is transferred to the owner, thus lessening by this amount his taxable income derived from his job.
3. The buyer has paid off approximately $800 on the principal during the year.
4. The property has, in fact, appreciated to, say, $129,600 (8%)

OR

Appreciation	$9,600
Reduction of principle	800
Net income	1,000
Tax savings on ordinary income (45% bracket)	900
	$12,300

By benefiting from inflation through the leveraging of real estate and by exploiting the difference between an accounting loss and an economic gain, the investor has not only improved his economic state but reduced his taxes. Since depreciation is based on the total value of the building rather than the original investment (down payment), it is not unusual for the investor's tax savings from the depreciation deduction to exceed his down payment in three to five years. *This is a tax shelter,* and since real estate can be bought in every conceivable price range, it is everyman's tax shelter. It makes as much sense to the rich as the not so rich.

As the investor depreciates his building, his adjusted basis declines. Assuming the same building is appreciating in value, then the investor is incurring an every-increasing capital gains liability. A capital gains tax of 25 percent of the "spread" will have to be paid upon the future sale of the building. However, the tax is deferred and deferring any expense is, in itself, an advantage. A current dollar is worth more than any future dollar and a current dollar can be reinvested in order to give an additional return.

The following chart may help clarify what a dollar is worth when time becomes a factor. Let us assume that a current dollar can be invested at 9 percent. Here is what a promise to pay a dollar at some future date is worth today.

Promise of $1.00 in	Today's Deferred Value
5 years	$.65
10 years	$.42
15 years	$.27
20 years	$.18

Since depreciation is a tax-deductible expense that requires no current cash expenditure, it creates a "paper" loss that can be used to offset income from other sources and it effectively shifts earnings from ordinary income to capital gains or to a much lower tax rate.

There are two other methods of depreciation in addition to the straight-line method previously discussed—the "sum of the years digits" and the "declining balance" methods. The former is applicable only to new construction, while the latter is applicable to both new construction and existing. In both cases, depreciation is greatest in the first years of ownership. A progressively smaller allowance is allowed each year.

A switch to the straight-line method may be accomplished any time during ownership but a switch from straight-line to the accelerated methods is not normally allowed. Therefore, it is in the investor's interest to use the schedule that gives him the maximum deduction in the early years of ownership and then switch to the straight-line method in the year the straight-line (if it was used) exceeds the accelerated methods.

With the passage of time, the tax-shelter benefits of real estate erode. This is due to increased rents, a decreasing percentage of your monthly payment devoted to interest (more to principal) and, if depreciation is deducted on an accelerated basis, the decreasing depreciation allowance. One way to restore the tax shelter is to refinance. The loan proceeds, unlike sale proceeds, are tax free.

A method of deferring capital gains is an exchange for similar or "like kind" property. This is a trade and has no capital gains consequences. This makes good sense on paper but in practice is very difficult. The two properties to be traded are rarely of the same fair market value. Since one is worth more than the other, someone has to trade up and someone has to trade down. The world is full of investors willing to expand and short on those willing to contract.

An investor may sell his property on a land contract (purchase-money mortgage). With this device, the seller is holding the mortgage and his capital gains are spread out over the life of the contract. The advantage to this is that a little tax damage per year is preferable to a lot of damage in one year.

RECORDKEEPING

It is essential that records be kept on any economic transaction that affects your home or income property. Closing statements, repair bills, improvement costs, bank statements and operating expenses determine not only your income but your adjusted bases.

In any audit, the burden of proof is on the taxpayer and the IRS does not accept "cross my heart and hope to die."

DEALER STATUS

In any area of real estate investment, care must be taken to avoid having the IRS consider you a dealer. A rapid buying and selling of real estate at a profit indicates that you are in the business of handling real estate and your property is considered inventory rather than a capital asset. You then lose long-term capital-gain tax advantages and are instead taxed at the ordinary rate. In this case, you are no better off than if you worked for a living.

SOCIAL SECURITY

Due to a declining birth rate, increased life expectancy, high unemployment and ever-increasing benefits, the social security system in 1977 was facing bankruptcy. In order to bail the system out, Congress passed the largest tax increase of any kind in the history of the earth: $227 billion over ten years.

The following chart will illustrate this dramatic increase.

Year	Yearly Wage Subject to Tax	Maximum Tax Paid by Employee/Employer	Dollar Increase	Percentage of Wages
1949	$ 3,000	$ 30.00	—	1
1959	4,800	120.00	$ 90.00	2.5
1969	7,800	374.40	254.40	4.8
1979	22,900	1403.77	1,029.37	6.13
1987	42,600	3045.90	1,642.13	7.15

In terms of total dollars spent, in 1970 a trifling $39 billion was spent on benefits; in 1979, $135 billion and by 1985 (hold on) $250 billion will be spent.

It is estimated that by the year 2000, the top social security tax on a worker will be over $7,000. This reflects the facts that by then there will be one beneficiary for every two workers (there are currently three workers for every beneficiary) and social security payments rise automatically with wage increases.

In addition, the amount deducted from the worker's paycheck is matched by the employer and this company expense is passed on to the consumer, therefore the wage earner pays twice. This fact alone may account for a .5 percent rise in the inflation rate for 1979.

Many low- and middle-income workers now pay more social security tax than income tax and the percentage of those in this situation will increase dramatically through the eighties. Assuming you'll be around to enjoy your sixty-fifth birthday (27.2 percent of you won't—sorry) and assuming you don't choose to work, you'll collect something between $1,461.60 and $5,876.40 per year. This kind of income can do little more than finance your bad habits. On the other hand, if you are 25 years old and both you and your employer contributed to a pension plan (at the same level you contribute to social security) yielding 7.5 percent compounded, on your sixty-fifth birthday you could expect to receive a lump-sum check of approximately $1.25 million. The interest income (8 percent) on this sum would be $100,000 per year.

The social security system is nothing more than a compulsory national chain letter, and if you're less than middle age you're at the bottom of the list.

Social security has absolutely nothing to do with real estate and it is this fact that will make real estate increasingly attractive. In order to ease the increasing social security burden, the modern investor should so structure his finances as to receive as much possible income or increase in net worth from capital gains or rent. This type of passive income, unlike earned income (wages and salaries), is immune from the social security drain. Real estate investment is the best method for avoiding this tax.

THE TAX AUDIT

Each year, one in fifty taxpayers is audited. However, the higher your income, the greater your chances of being audited. You also increase your chances of an audit if your tax return is unusual in comparison with others in your income bracket. This doesn't mean you are guilty of anything. It may only mean you are unusual.

Should you be audited, it's important to be calm and cooperative. It's not a legal proceeding but you would do well to be on your court behavior. This consists of volunteering nothing. Answer concisely only those questions asked of you. This is not an audition for Miss America. You are not obliged to be entertaining or profound. You may bring your accountant or tax lawyer with you and should something go wrong, you have an appeal procedure starting with your district conferee. Ultimately, your case may go to court.

In my opinion, if you have never been audited, you have probably been paying too much.

There are only two ways a taxpayer can err when filing his taxes: He may underestimate his income or he may overestimate his deductions. Underestimating one's income beyond a certain percentage, say 25 percent, can be construed as fraud, which can best be atoned for in the penitentiary. Overestimating deductions, if you're caught, results in paying the difference plus a penalty.

SUMMARY

The federal government is the largest debtor, creditor, employer, landholder and lawgiver in the history of the galaxy. Therefore, no investment book is complete without a discussion of politics, politicians and political trends. It must be included not only in the narrative but must be the point of departure from which all else develops.

Politics, inflation, financing and taxes are not separate entities but part of a package deal. This fluid and ambiguous composite formed by these diverse inputs, when coupled with local market knowledge, forms the investment mentality.

The nature of the politician is to please. He defines pleasing as giving and giving what you don't have is inflationary. Since inflation (a subtle robbery) can easily be blamed on others, he has the best of both worlds, do-gooderism and lack of blame for the consequences.

The only successful antidote to inflation is a leveraged investment in a durable good. And since real estate is the most leverage-able of investments you really have no better choice.

And finally, our tax code favors the real estate investor by means of the depreciation deduction and a favorable long-term capital gains tax. While hard work builds character, it doesn't build great fortunes. It's taxed too dearly. Great wealth now blesses the smart investor.

And yet, understanding these factors without understanding change is to miss the point. The only sure thing about real estate is constant change. Taxes, interest rates, financing terms, real estate law, prices, utility costs, tax law, tastes and even what is considered a desirable location are in a continual state of flux.

The reader is advised to disregard every number he sees in this book. The cost of real estate and its terms is relative to time and place. Today, a bi-level selling for $60,000 may be realistic in certain areas but in the future this figure may make sense only to those shopping for a respectable five-piece bedroom set.

The purpose of the preceding chapters is not to tattoo numbers on your brain, but to provide you with an anchorage from which you can measure, calculate, plot, think, scheme, weigh, choose, ponder and in every other way make the best possible investment choice.

I hope that by reading this book you are able to get your hands firmly around the golden goose from which the golden eggs will forever drop. This golden goose is not a system of numbers but an investment psychology, applicable not only to real estate but many other forms of investment. It is your job to keep current with the ever-changing recipe for this stew.

If, however, you use this book as a treasure map to the X, you will have initial success but your long-term investment future is doubtful.

Ponzi's World is a movable feast and offers everything except consistency.

CHAPTER 6

APPRAISAL

An appraisal is a hunch based on experience and varnished with two coats of mathematics.

—Author

*A*ppraising is an art not a science. It is an approximation of truth rather than truth defined. Although it is only an educated guess, at least it has the distinction of being educated. The alternative is a primal judgment spasm, which is of concern only to political pollsters.

All buyers, sellers and renters unwittingly perform an appraising function. Their results are strictly judgmental and, as such, are sometimes off the mark. This is particularly true when appraising income property. The purpose of this chapter is to give mathematical justification to what may or may not be a correct judgment.

VALUE

There are many types of value that can be assigned to real estate: loan value, insurable value, mortgage loan value, salvage value, rental value, assessed value or fair market value. It is with fair market value that we will be concerned and this may be defined as the price which a ready, willing, able and informed seller will accept and a ready, willing, able and informed buyer will pay (assuming the property is exposed on the market for a reasonable time).

It is important to know that value is not necessarily the same as cost or price. Value is an estimate of future benefit, while cost represents past expenditure. For example, given two identical homes, one located close to an industrial plant and the other in a desirable residential area, each would require the same cost to reproduce but would have different market values.

Price represents only the amount paid for the property, but due to an overanxious seller or uninformed buyer may be higher or lower than market value.

APPRAISING RESIDENTIAL PROPERTY

All residential property is part of a larger market. A suitable synonym for market may be "neighborhood." The boundaries of a neighborhood or market may be determined by a number of factors: a political subdivision (city, county), natural boundaries (rivers, lakes, mountains, swamps), man-made boundaries (railroads, highways, canals), ethnic homogeneity or architectural style. These perimeters, however determined, are intuitively known by the inhabitants.

Homes are valued in relation to their own market. Many factors contribute to making one market more desirable than another. Some of these include:

1. Proximity to a major labor market
2. Quality of schools
3. Transportation
4. Recreational and amusement facilities
5. Cultural and religious institutions
6. City services
7. Architectural tastes
8. Local construction costs

It can therefore be said that much of what constitutes the value of a home is of an external nature. A run-down home in a highly desirable residential market may be worth more than its well-maintained counterpart in a market considered undesirable.

There are thousands of markets in the United States and each has its own characteristics. This local nature of real estate defies bigness. Large corporations or investment groups can't possibly master the characteristics of all markets. It is precisely due to this local nature of real estate that opportunity will always be present for the small- and medium-size real estate investor. Like the local saloonkeeper, only he can understand all the intricacies of his market.

There are three methods used to appraise real estate: the cost approach, the sales comparison approach and the income approach. With existing single-family residences, the sales comparison approach is employed. This method gives an indication of value by comparing the property with recent sales and offerings of similar properties within your market.

THE SALES COMPARISON APPROACH

Information on recent sales is available from your local real estate agent. All real estate firms keep a "comp" file on all sold properties within their market. These data sheets not only describe the physical characteristics of the property in detail but give the actual sale price, length of time on the market and, frequently, the terms under which the home was financed by the new buyer.

Since no two properties can ever be the same, upward or downward adjustments must be made between the comps and the property being appraised. The following are things to look for in comps:

1. Whether personal property was included in the sale.
2. Whether there has been a price increase or decrease since the date of the sale.
3. The terms of financing the sale (an FHA or VA sale generally results in a higher sale price due to seller discount points).
4. The degree of preservation.
5. The location of the property within the neighborhood.

Once you've selected three properties most comparable to the one you're appraising, they can then be adjusted to indicate the present value of the subject property.

After averaging the prices in the table on page 89, a final appraisal figure of $58,500 should result.

The same sales comparison approach is used to determine the value of a vacant lot. Other than location, depth of the lot is frequently a variable. In an area with a standard lot depth, deeper lots are worth more than shallow; however, the front part of the lot is worth more than the rear part. In order to determine how much the value of the lot is decreased by shallower variations from the standard depth, the 4–3–2–1 thumb rule is frequently used.

Appraisal date June 1, 1979	Comp 1	Comp 2	Comp 3
Sales price	$ 51,000	$ 54,500	$ 56,000
Date of sale	Jan. 1, 1978	June 1, 1978	May 1, 1979
Date of sale adjustment (assuming a 10% rate of appreciation)	+ 7,905	+ 5,450	+ 560
Location within the neighborhood (property 2 bordered on a park)	0	− 1,000	0
Personal property (property 1 included range and refrigerator)	− 500	0	0
Maintenance (property 3 needed complete outside painting and landscaping —needed upgrading in order to conform with the rest of the neighborhood)	0	0	+ 1,500
Net adjustment	+ 7,405	+ 4,450	+ 2,060
Indicated value of subject property	$58,405	$ 58,950	$ 58,060

THE 4–3–2–1 RULE

40% of a lot's total value is assigned to the front 25%
30% of a lot's total value is assigned to the next 25%
20% of a lot's total value is assigned to the next 25%
10% of a lot's total value is assigned to the rear 25%

The standard lot in a neighborhood is 75 feet by 160 feet and sells for $18,000. By employing the 4–3–2–1 rule, the value may be allocated:

Front 40 feet	$7,200 (40%)
Next 40 feet	5,400 (30%)
Next 40 feet	3,600 (20%)
Rear 40 feet	1,800 (10%)
160 foot depth	$18,000 (100%)

From this, it can be deduced that a shallower lot of 120 feet would be worth $16,200 ($7,200 + $5,400 + $3,600).

You are cautioned against using this or any other thumb rule in this book as a substitute for a thorough investigation of the property. Each parcel of real estate is unique and all thumb rules are generalizations. This paradox is tolerated only because thumb rules are an easy and quick way to arrive at a common denominator. They also make you appear smart. If, in the above example, the rear quarter of the lot bordered on a recreational lake or was too shallow to be buildable, then the thumb rule would be useless. The only inviolable thumb rule I can think of is "Don't stick your thumb in a meat grinder."

DISTANCE TO FACILITIES

The following table lists the ideal, maximum distances to daily activities for homeowners in urban areas. In many cases, commuting time may be more important than actual distance. When evaluating property, some consideration should be given to these safe recommendations, but keep in mind these rules are only guides.

Facility	Ideal Maximum Distance
Local shopping center	.75 mile
Grade school	1 mile
High school	2.5 miles
Churches and recreational facilities	3.5 miles
Major shopping center	4 miles
Employment	40 minutes

LIFE CYCLES

All neighborhoods pass through three distinct stages during their life cycles. The first stage is one of development. This construction stage may last 10 to 15 years. After this stage, when few vacant sites remain, the neighborhood is said to be in a state of equilibrium. It is during this stage that homes tend to be at their highest value. The last stage of the cycle is one of decline. This is caused by the general deterioration of housing in the area. For this reason, and in the absence of any particular market preference, the investor is advised to select property in the path of city expansion. This point is not all-important since the period of equilibrium may last 50 years or more. Nevertheless, the investor should give some consideration to a neighborhood's stage in its life cycle and buy in adolescence or middle age and not in the approach of senility. However, since land is limited and indestructible, the death of a neighborhood signals its eventual rebirth, at which time the cycle begins anew.

RESIDENTIAL CONSTRUCTION

While a complete discussion of construction techniques is beyond the scope of this book, a general knowledge of construction can not only help the investor determine the quality of any particular building but help him spot various flaws.

Wood frame construction is currently the most commonly used method of building single-family homes. The advantages to this type of construction are not only cost, but less building time, ease of insulation and, most of all, greater flexibility in design.

While there is no official national building code, FHA and VA standards tend to influence all local codes in regard to materials, structural strength, safety, and sanitary construction.

Recent trends in subdivision construction have stressed exterior variations and minor style changes while adhering to the same basic house. This allows the builder to take advantage of economics of scale and at the same time offer enough differentiation to lend an individuality to each of his homes. For example, a colonial becomes a Dutch colonial by substituting a gambrel roof for a gable roof.

FOUNDATION

Foundations support the home and may be constructed of cut stone, stone and brick, concrete or concrete block. Concrete, with steel reinforcing rods, is the preferred material for foundation walls due to its strength and moisture-resistant characteristics. The type and cost of a foundation depend on soil quality. Poor soil bearing conditions (too soft) require the sinking of piles or a home built on a rock ledge (too hard) requires blasting. Both add to foundation costs and are a negative entry when appraising a vacant lot.

Homes without basements are built on a concrete slab foundation and homes with a crawl space generally employ a pier and beam foundation. A pier is a vertical, steel-reinforced concrete column used to support the horizontal beam.

In your inspection of a concrete foundation, hairline cracks can be overlooked, but wider vertical cracks may indicate settling with the result of doors not closing properly, cracked walls and squeaking floors. In a cement or cinder-block foundation, crumbling mortar indicates too high a ratio of sand in the mix.

Check for water stains on the basement wall and make sure the basement floor slopes to a drain for easy runoff.

FRAMING

The frame or skeleton of the house is the next to be fabricated and erected. Two-by-four vertical studs—spaced not in excess of 24 inches apart on a one-story house and not in excess of 16 inches on a two-story house—rest on a sill, which is secured to the foundation wall or slab.

Two types of wall frame construction are in general use—platform frame and balloon frame. In the platform method, the frame is constructed on a floor-by-floor basis, whereas in the balloon method, the studs are continuous from foundation to the ceiling of the second floor. The preferred method and most frequently used is the platform frame.

The sheathing, or lining, is then nailed directly to the wall studs. Sheathing may be pine, fiber insulating board, plywood or paper-covered gypsum. Wood, aluminum or vinyl siding is then nailed up to form the outside wall. Older homes are sometimes renovated by re-siding with asphalt or asbestos shingles. Brick or stone veneer is commonly used to cover a frame home in order to give it the appearance of a solid brick or stone home. You can tell a veneered-frame home from a solid-masonry home by the thickness of the wall. Veneered homes' walls never exceed 8 inches while a masonry home is never less than 10 inches in thickness.

I see no particular advantage to a solid-masonry construction as it is expensive, a poor insulator, is susceptible to water seepage and its beauty can be duplicated with veneer.

Insulation is then placed between the studs. The insulation material is either of rock wool or fiberglass and with or without an aluminum vapor barrier.

WINDOWS AND DOORS

Windows and exterior doors follow in the construction sequence. Windows come in five basic styles:

1. Single-hung window—opens vertically, has one movable sash, usually the bottom.
2. Double-hung window—opens vertically from the top and bottom, containing two separate sashes with a locking device, usually at the center, where the top of the lower sash meets the bottom of the upper sash.
3. Traverse window—has sashes which open horizontally, sliding on separate grooves parallel to each other.
4. Casement window—has hinges on its sides, allowing it to swing open vertically.
5. Jalousie window—has adjustable, horizontal glass slats which keep out the sun or rain while letting in the light and air.

Double-glazed windows, with an air space between the two sheets of glass, are the most energy-efficient type of window for all parts of the country.

Door construction is either panel, hollow core, solid core or louver. The materials used are typically mahogany, birch, walnut or oak in thicknesses $1\frac{3}{8}$" (interior) and $1\frac{3}{4}$" (exterior). Steel- or aluminum-framed sliding glass doors are currently popular for the exit to a patio or backyard.

ROOF

Roofs are described either as conventional (assembled on site) or truss (assembled in a plant and set in place by a crane). A truss roof can be distinguished by "W"-shaped supports for the rafters. Rafters (the load-bearing timbers of a roof which establish its slope) should be either 2 by 6 inches spaced 16 inches apart or 2 by 8 inches spaced 24 inches apart. Currently, the most popular roof covering is asphalt strip shingles over tar-felt building paper. Flashing is the metal strip (copper or sheet lead) used to make a watertight union in any break in the roof such as around the chimney. Aluminum is the most popular material currently used in gutters and downspouts.

PLUMBING, HEATING, AIR CONDITIONING AND ELECTRICAL

Fresh-water pipes are made of copper, brass or plastic (copper is best) and sanitary drains are made of cast iron or plastic. Hot water is generally heated by electricity, gas or oil. The size of the water heater is important. A water heater with a capacity of less than 40 gallons is unsuitable for a family of four. Fiberglass and porcelain-coated cast iron or steel are the materials used for plumbing fixtures.

A forced-air heating system is the most popular in use today. The air is heated by gas, electricity or oil and a blower motor distributes the air via sheet-metal ducts throughout the house. An air conditioner, humidifier, dehumidifier or electronic air cleaner may be made an integral part of this system. Other types of heating systems in use are electric radiant, steam, hot water and the heat pump.

Due to the increased use of electrical appliances and gadgets, the modern home should have an increased amount of wall outlets, switches and circuits. The circuit-breaker box is replacing the fuse box as a distribution for home electric service.

INTERIOR WALLS AND FLOORS

Plaster board, ⅜ inches thick, has replaced plaster walls in all but the most expensive residential construction. Cost considerations have made this so and I think it is an entirely suitable substitute. It gives a smooth, plasterlike surface and, unlike plaster, doesn't crack. You can tell the difference between plaster and dry wall by tapping the wall. A hollow sound indicates dry-wall construction.

Due to increasing costs, oak, maple, hard pine and fir strips are being phased out in all but the higher-priced homes in favor of plywood floors. This plywood is covered with wall-to-wall carpeting, linoleum or ceramic, vinyl, asphalt or vinyl asbestos tile.

When checking interior walls, look for open joints in trim and baseboards, warping and nail popping. Protruding nails in dry wall indicate insufficiently dried lumber used for the studs. As you walk the floors, be on the lookout for sloping and squeaking. Make sure all doors and windows open, close and latch easily. And finally, check for water stains around the windows.

USEFUL LIFE

All building systems and components have useful lives or a time period beyond which repair is uneconomical. For example, the average home heater expected to last twenty years may, in fact, perform for fifteen or thirty years depending on the degree of usage and preventive maintenance. Or more probably, it lasts fifteen or thirty years because it's just one of those things. In all respects, it is not much different than the human heart.

The table on page 97 not only gives average life spans but, in many cases, correctly assumes you get what you pay for. It will assist you in appraising a building or, if you currently own it, making the decision to repair or replace.

Since plumbing fixtures are long-lived items, it is frequently the case that they become obsolete for style long before they deteriorate beyond repair. For example, separate hot- and cold-water faucets, as opposed to one mixing faucet, are stylistically obsolete in spite of their reliability.

THE COST APPROACH

In many ways, the sales comparison approach to residential appraising is the best as it relies on recent proven sales of like homes. However, this approach cannot be used when no recent sales are available or when the property to be appraised is unique. Also, since no two properties are exactly the same, this method suffers from the appraiser's "guesstimate" of value due to differences between similar properties.

	Low Qual.	Avg. Qual.	Good Qual.	Excellent
Air conditioner	10 (years)	12 (years)	15 (years)	17 (years)
Range and refrigerator	10	12	14	16
Garbage disposal	6	7	9	12
Water heater	2	5	8	12
Heating plants	12	15	20	25
Light fixtures		15		
Wiring		20		
Plumbing faucets and valves		15–20		
Fixtures (tubs and bowls)		25		
Iron cold-water pipes		25		
Iron hot-water pipes		20		
Roofs:				
Asbestos		25		
Tar and gravel		20		
Tile		40		
Asphalt		20		
Wells and well pumps		25		
Window screens		10		
Awnings		5		

With the cost approach, the appraiser tries to determine the cost of reproducing any building and, in so doing, takes into account depreciation.

The formula is simple:

Reproduction Cost − Building Depreciation + Land Value
= Property Value of Building

An additional reason for using the cost approach is to verify results obtained from the sales comparison method.

The easiest way to find the reproduction cost of any building is to check the price per square foot of new construction offered in the area. In any market subject to a single building code, a dollar-per-square-foot figure is easily arrived at. Currently, and in the market with which I am most familiar, a two-story can be built for approximately $35 per square foot. I arrived at this figure by calling three builders and averaging their quotes.

A problem does develop when appraising an older home. Economically unduplicatable workmanship such as stained-glass windows and plaster walls may require that the appraiser figure the replacement cost versus the reproduction cost. The replacement cost is the cost of reproducing a building having the same utility (the same number of bedrooms, baths, etc.).

All buildings depreciate in three ways:

1. Physical deterioration is the wear and tear of the building's structure and its systems (electrical, heating, plumbing) due to time and usage.

2. Functional obsolescence is the need for modernization due to the ever-changing tastes and demands of the home buyer. For example, a small master bedroom unable to accommodate a king-size bed and other heroic furniture, absence of a first-floor family room, one bath instead of at least one and a half, an awkward floor plan, dated fixtures and, in many markets, a one-car garage, while tolerable 30 years ago, are obsolete today.

3. Economic obsolescence is the loss of value due to reasons external to the property. For example, a zoning change that brings

industrial activity into a residential area will have a negative effect on the property.

The following is an application of the cost approach appraisal method. Let us assume that:

1. Construction costs average $30 per square foot in a particular market.

2. The useful life of a single-family residence is 60 years.

3. A site value of $30,000 is arrived at by using the sales comparison approach.

4. A 10-year-old, 2,000-square-foot building is to be appraised.

THEN

Reproduction Cost of Building — Building Depreciation + land value = property value

(2,000 sq. ft. $\times$ $30) − (2,000 sq. ft. $\times$ 30 $\times$ 1/6) + $30,000 = Property Value

$60,000 − $10,000 + $30,000 = $80,000

INCOME APPROACH

The income approach of appraising is the most common method of valuing income-producing property such as an apartment building. This method assumes that a ratio exists within any given market between the cost of a building and its income.

The "gross rent multiplier" is the best method used to determine value of income property via this approach. If we were to use an apartment building as an example, our first step would be to determine a ratio for the building's particular market between gross monthly rent and sales price. Gross monthly income is nothing more than total monthly rent. Operating expenses, debt repayment or income from a coin laundry is not considered. Past sales of apartment buildings in the area would be our data source. This ratio is expressed mathematically as:

Sales Price $\div$ Gross Monthly Rent = Gross Rent Multiplier

Sale	Sales Price	÷	Monthly Gross Rent	=	Gross Rent Mult.
#1 (6 units)	$182,000		$ 1,600		$ 113.75
#2 (4 units)	133,000		1,150		115.65
#3 (3 units)	88,500		765		115.68
#4 (8 units)	220,000		1,925		114.29

In the above example, the average gross rent multiplier is 114.8 for the area. This would indicate that a five-unit apartment building with a gross monthly rent of $1,125 would be worth $129,000 ($1,125 × 114.8 = $129,000).

Since higher rents create a higher sales price, the G.R.M. tends to be a constant, or when it does change in response to market conditions, it changes rather slowly. Nothing in real estate can be viewed as a constant, but the G.R.M. is more constant than both rents and sales prices.

Another method of establishing value on a multifamily building is to use market data of comparable buildings to establish a price per unit. If the average unit price in your area is $22,500, then an eight-unit apartment building should sell for $180,000.

CAPITALIZATION RATE

This method of determining value, while it claims a noble past, has now fallen into a state of disrepute. I discuss it not because it is of any importance, but because the reason for its unimportance *is important.* To put it another way, understanding why prohibition was repealed tells you more about human nature than understanding why it was enacted.

The "cap" rate assumes that any investor has an investment alternative. He may invest, say, $22,000 in a high-grade (safe) bond yielding 9 percent or in real estate (equally safe). But since real estate is a non-liquid investment and requires some management effort, he chooses, say, 11 percent as his desired return.

Therefore, if he knows the *net* income of any investment, he can determine its value by dividing it by his desired return ("cap rate").

If we assume the net income of a real estate investment is $22,000 and the investor's desired cap rate is 11 percent:

THEN

$$\frac{\text{Net Income}}{\text{Capitalization Rate}} = \text{Value}$$

OR

$$\frac{\$22,000}{11\% \ (.11)} = \$200,000$$

OR TRANSPOSED

$$\frac{\text{Net Income}}{\text{Value}} = \text{Capitalization Rate}$$

$$\frac{\$22,000}{\$ \ 200,000} = 11\%$$

OR TRANSPOSED

Capitalization Rate X Value = Net Income

$11\% \times \$200,000 \quad = \quad \$22,000$

This type of income approach, while philosophically sound, has become tactically sloppy.

Real estate is unique and cannot be measured against any other investment. Small- and medium-sized investors recognize this. In recent years the motive of the real estate investor has changed from income to appreciation and tax shelter. In addition, in many major markets no seller or buyer can exchange an apartment building without considering its future conversion to a condominium. Both are upward pressures on price and therefore downward pressures on the cap rate. This change of investor motive has forced income property into a price range which reduces the cap rate to a meaningless figure. In many cases, it is a minus figure.

I have personally sold many properties to investors that have shown negative incomes in the early years of ownership. Until rents can be raised to match expenses, the investor is in the red. The primary reason this situation is endured is tax shelter.

Due to this change in investor motive, an interesting corollary follows: *rents have never been lower.*

In noninflationary dollars, rent expressed as a percentage of building value is low. The following example from my own experience may help illustrate this point.

TWO-BEDROOM TOWN HOUSE

	Rent	Value	$\dfrac{\text{Sale Price}}{\text{Monthly Gross Income}}$ = G.R.M.
1971	$195 per mo.	$22,000	112.8
1979	$325 per mo.	$55,000	169.2

In this example, the rent as expressed in terms of building value has been halved in spite of a $130 increase in eight years.

USING THE VALUE APPROACHES

The sales comparison approach is the best method of appraising residential property. The cost approach may be used to verify the result or it can be used to appraise a unique building. The income approach is used to appraise income property and should also be verified by the cost approach.

Appraising of residential property is an estimation of buyer impulse. The mathematics is easy and serves to define the upper and lower limits of value within a few percent. However, a fine tuning can be achieved only with judgment. This judgment or "feel" is an intangible. Football handicappers invoke the intangibles in their prophesies and they're frequently correct—why not appraisers? If I were sure of what the intangibles were, they would not be intangible, therefore the following is a guess.

The appearance of spaciousness may account for an upward price adjustment of as much as 5 percent. Light colors, a minimum amount of furniture and minimumly covered windows give an appearance of spaciousness. Unfortunately, most homes do not have this spacious feel.

It is safe to say that after 15 years of marriage, enough furniture is bought and inherited to crowd the typical home. To add to this problem, the recent tendency to "get back to our roots" by acquiring dreadnought-sized antiques only aggravates the situation. Velvet drapes, red flocked wallpaper, ponderous lamps, uncountable knickknacks and other whorehouse manifestations finish the job.

Decor is important, but I suspect a *uniformity* of decor is more important. Most homes are furnished as money becomes available. For this reason, the style of furnishings represent the buyer's mood at the time of purchase. Since tastes change with time, most of our homes lack coherence in decor.

All homes 40 years of age or older (unless remodeled) are plagued with a certain amount of functional obsolescence. Small kitchens and bedrooms, no family room or the presence of barbaric bathrooms are some of the problems. And yet, as we discussed before, these homes frequently display a workmanship reflecting an age in which it took more than a union card to call oneself a carpenter. The degree to which workmanship atones for functional obsolescence is an intangible.

The advantage of owning a corner lot has a place only in American mythology. Currently, I see no advantage to a corner lot. Traffic on two sides of the home and small backyards, in most cases, do not outweigh any privacy advantages in having only one neighbor.

OPTIONS

Refining your appraising skills and becoming an expert in your market can have a favorable economic fallout. By using the option, an investor whose knowledge far exceeds his cash reserves can turn a profit by exploiting certain market irregularities.

An option is a right, which has the effect of a continuing offer, given for a consideration (money), to purchase or lease property at an agreed-upon price and terms within a specified time.

Here is how an option works in practice. Assume you find a parcel of land zoned commercial in your area for sale at $80,000.

Let us also assume that you spot a trend of franchise fast-food firms developing in the area. If you're willing to take some risk, you can take an option to buy the property within six months for $80,000 with, let's say, $2,000 as an option price. If within six months' time you are unable to find a buyer for the property willing to pay a price in excess of $80,000, you lose your $2,000. However, if you can sell the property for, say, $95,000, the difference (minus selling expenses) is yours.

This is a good game for those with a thorough market knowledge, including contacts with potential buyers. It does not require a great deal of cash and satisfies any gambling urge the investor may have.

I am reminded of the story of a young man who had difficulty parking at his local chain food store. He noticed a dilapidated home next to the store and optioned the property for $500 for six months at a sales price of $15,000. He then complained to the store manager of the parking problem in the area. On the following day, his wife whinnied the same complaint. On the third day, the chain store offered the optionee $25,000 for the adjacent property.

CHAPTER 7

YOUR OWN HOME

We shape our dwellings,
and afterwards our dwellings shape us.
—Winston Churchill

*Y*our own home is your most important single investment. It not only gives shelter and stability to your life but in time becomes a source of security. If you bought your home five years ago, the chances are it has grown in value to such an extent that you could not afford to buy it today. For most people, their homes are not only their largest single investment but the equity in them has become the largest single determinant of their net worth. Because of this, I do not distinguish between a home buyer and real estate investor. Whether buying your own primary residence or property you intend to rent, it's an investment.

REAL ESTATE VS. PERSONAL PROPERTY

All things that can be owned are either real estate or personal property. Real estate is defined as the earth's surface including the permanent additions, made by man or nature, as well as the air above and the earth below. Personal property is anything that does not fit this definition. It's important to know the difference as each is subject to a different set of laws. For example, the deed is the instrument used to convey real estate whereas a bill of sale conveys personal property. The following examples may help clarify the difference between real estate and personal property.

Real Estate	*Personal Property*
Land	Furniture
House	Mobile home
Wall-to-Wall tacked-down carpeting	Area rug
Chandelier	Swag lamp
Tree	Same tree cut for firewood
Built-in dishwasher	Portable dishwasher
In-ground swimming pool	Above-ground pool
Central air conditioner	Window air conditioner

For a buyer or seller, unless there is an agreement to the contrary, a real estate contract transfers real estate only.

106

THE BUYER AS COMPROMISER

The French have a saying: "To live is to choose." This is never more important than when selecting a home. Every buyer, whether he wants to or not, becomes a compromiser. Unless he has unlimited wealth, a buyer sooner or later comes to the realization that he must pay more, accept a lesser house or a less desirable location in order to be an owner.

Any realtor will tell you that location is the most important single factor in home selection and it is that factor which the buyer should least compromise. This makes good sense. You can always rehabilitate a run-down home, add a family room or stretch your housing budget, but you cannot change your building site.

SELLING YOUR HOME

The only advantage in avoiding a real estate firm when selling your property is avoiding the sales commission. I blanch at the simplicity of this statement. And yet, a thorough understanding of the nature of the commission is not widely known.

To begin with, the typical commission adds up to a lot of money. (Three to six thousand dollars on a $60,000 home.) It is interesting to note that the *true* sales commission, as expressed in terms of your equity, is higher than you may think. It is always higher than the realty firm thinks. If we take the typical 35-year-old, middle-income seller as an example, we may find his total equity in his $60,000 home to be something like $25,000. And keep in mind that the commission is based on the sale price of the home and not the equity. A sales commission of 7 percent translates to 16.8 percent in terms of his home investment. And when you consider that the average seller's equity represents the largest portion of his net worth (total assets minus total liabilities), you realize that the commission may represent 10 percent of all the seller ever worked for! This fact alone should encourage you to *demand* first-class service from your broker. Periodic reports from your salesman on the status of your home, frequent and professional advertising are not outrageous seller demands.

Commission rates vary according to local custom and fall between 5 percent and 10 percent of the sale price of your home. It is important to note that the law states that the commission rate is determined by negotiations between seller and broker. Therefore, no harm can be done by offering to pay the broker 5 percent instead of 7 percent. The more expensive your home, the easier it is to get your broker to "give." He understands that no more effort is required in selling an expensive home as opposed to selling a cheaper one, yet the commission is higher.

There is a commission involved in the sale of every home and it makes no difference whether it is sold through a real estate firm or by the owner. The only question is who gets the commission. It could be the buyer, seller or realty firm or some combination of the three but, believe me, a commission is involved.

A recent national survey has shown that sellers, after all selling expenses are considered, do no better selling by owner as opposed to listing with a realty firm. It is important to note that this is a national average and has nothing to do with you in particular. The reason for this is interesting. *All* sellers have a fairly accurate idea of what their property is worth. It is within my own experience that they are 3 percent to 5 percent too high, but this is close enough. Many sellers ask a real estate salesman for a free appraisal solely in order to confirm what they already know. The seller then offers his home "for sale by owner" at a figure 7 percent to 10 percent in excess of the broker's recommendation. This is in keeping with the advice of all the cousin Harrys in the world who say "You can always come down."

The prospective buyer, upon learning the sales price, invariably subtracts the commission plus 3 percent to 4 percent because he can see no reason why he shouldn't be compensated for his house-seeking efforts and also in order to conform with cousin Harry's second dictum: "Always offer the seller 10 percent less than his asking price." Since the seller expects to be compensated for his advertising costs and salesmanship (a commission) and the buyer thinks this is ridiculous (he wants the commission) a 10 percent or more difference results between the buyer's offer and the seller's asking price. This is the unwritten commission as opposed to the real one the broker charges, but it is real nonetheless. The buyer's offer frequently results in netting the seller the same as what he would have netted by listing his home with a broker. The solution to this impass is mathematical since a just price can best be arrived at by the buyer and seller splitting the difference between their offers (splitting the commission). Unfortunately this is mathematics not reality. Buyers and sellers are frequently too adamant for this type of compromise.

Here is my advice on selling your home for the highest possible price, in the shortest possible time, with the minimum amount of fuss:

1. *Give yourself enough time.* In most markets four months seems to be ideal. Remember, it takes at least one month from the day a contract is signed to the closing day. This one-month period is the time it takes for your buyer to arrange for financing. Therefore you have only three months in which to sell your home.

2. *Try selling it yourself.* Should the seller have four months or longer in which to sell his home, I would strongly recommend he try selling it himself. The chances of your being successful are something like one out of five; however, in terms of cash, you don't have much to lose. A one-time charge of $10 for a sign and $30 per week for advertising is about average and is a good gamble, in spite of the odds, against thousands of dollars in commission. But remember the unwritten commission (discount) that the buyer expects to collect. Your biggest risk in selling your own home is time, and time is money.

Here is an example of how, in real estate, time easily converts to money. You buy a home to close on May 1. You also begin selling your home by owner on February 1. Your price is too high but "you can always come down" and on March 15 you do. If your home is not sold by April 1, the specter of owning two homes concurrently haunts you. Therefore you drop your price still further. This time you're asking less than the fair market value of your home.

LISTING AGREEMENTS

Should you decide to sell property through a real estate agency, you will be asked to sign a listing agreement. This is nothing more than an employment contract. An agency relationship then exists in which the seller is the principal (boss) and the broker is the agent (employee). This is also a relationship of trust in which the broker owes obedience, accounting and, above all, loyalty to the seller. There are four types of listing agreements in general use and I list them in order of importance.

1. Exclusive Right to Sell. With this type of listing only one broker is authorized to act as agent for the property. Under this agreement, the seller gives up the right to sell the property himself without being obligated to pay a commission. The broker frequently shares this type of listing with other brokerage firms in the area. This allows any broker to sell the property and receive a sales commission from your listing broker. This is a definite advantage to the seller as it increases the number of brokers with access to his property.

2. Exclusive Agency Listings. With this type of listing, only one broker is authorized to act as exclusive agent for the seller. The seller, however, retains the right to sell the property himself without obligation to the broker.

3. Open Listing. Under an open listing, the seller may employ any number of brokers to act as agents. The seller is obligated to pay a commission only to the broker who brings about a sale and he reserves the right to sell the property himself without a commission obligation.

4. Net Listing. With this type of listing, the seller informs the broker as to what he wants to receive for his property. The broker is then free to offer the property for sale at any higher price he wants. Upon the sale of the property, the broker pays to the seller the net amount and keeps the remainder as his commission. This type of listing is illegal in many states and is not recommended in the others.

All listings must be in writing and:

1. Precisely describe the real estate listed.
2. State price and other terms.
3. Describe the commission.
4. Signed by the seller and the broker.

While oral listings are allowed in many states, they are not advisable for either the broker or seller due to the potential for dispute regarding terms. Most brokers have a policy of not accepting oral listings as it puts their commission on a handshake basis. In the past, this type of relationship has frequently meant sell and sue for the broker and neither he nor the seller need this aggravation.

As an agent of the seller, the broker is obliged to exercise his best efforts to sell his listed property including active advertising. He is bound not to disclose any information given to him in confidence and he cannot buy for his own account any properties offered for sale without the seller's full knowledge. He must submit all buyer offers for his listings and must follow all *legal* instructions of the seller.

The best listing for the broker and seller is the "exclusive right to sell" as all others are half measures. This type of listing gives the broker the best security and makes him work harder to bring about a sale. In many markets, it's the only type of listing that your broker is able to share with other brokers in the multiple-listing service.

The only disadvantage to this type of listing is that you forfeit your right to sell the property yourself without paying a commission; however, even this is not absolute. If, during your "by owner" period, you discussed your property with four potential buyers, you may list them on the listing agreement (by name) as exceptions to the listing contract. Should they buy within a specified period of time, say 10 days, you will avoid paying a commission. This has the additional advantage of forcing them into a decision. The more time you can get to allow your exceptions to buy the better your position. Forty-five days is ideal. Should your broker submit a written offer to buy within this 45-day period, you can then notify your exceptions. Tell them the amount and terms of your bona-fide offer. If your broker's offer is $70,000 with a 6 percent commission, your net before other selling expenses is $65,800. Should your exception buyer split the commission, you may sell your property to him for $67,900 and save half the commission. This is $2,100 extra in your pocket. With a combination of luck and skill, anyone can sell "by owner" and save a part of the commission, but no seller ever saves the whole commission.

Brokers do not like sellers who sell to their exceptions by using this ploy. They don't like hemorrhoids either but it "comes with the territory."

ESTABLISHING A PRICE

The first step in selling real estate is establishing a selling price. Every seller now knows the approximate value of his home. It's too important a source of the average homeowner's net worth not to be verified on a monthly basis. Homeowners now follow local real estate ads the way they once followed their stock prices. Nevertheless, a 5 percent error, high or low, can result in trouble for the seller in that it either takes too long to sell or is sold too quickly and at a discount. Also, since tens of thousands of dollars are involved, sellers need reassurance.

Unless your property is unusual, paying a real estate appraiser is an unnecessary expense. Any local experienced real estate salesman can give you the same figure at no charge. Ah, but will he give you the figure?

Real estate is currently the most competitive business in the United States, and within real estate, the pressure to list properties is intense. This type of competition requires people who ought to know better to resort to lying to the stupid and flattering the intelligent. In many markets this translates to the salesmen overestimating the value of your home in order to eliminate the competition who "don't think so big." The salesman tries to get his overpriced listing for as long as possible, knowing that inflation will catch up. An experienced salesman also knows that after six weeks the seller becomes more realistic and is apt to drop his price. He is also comforted in the old adage "They all sell someday."

A few unethical salesmen attempt to underestimate the value of the home in order to get a quick sale or buy it for his own account. In either case, the seller is not getting the truth.

Since an appraiser makes you pay for the truth, your best strategy is to work the truth out of the salesman for free. Here is how this is done. Ask the salesman for the truth. Tell him you're tired of ego trips. Most salesmen feel comfortable with this type of approach from the seller. This relieves the salesman of the drudgery of embroidering an unrealistically high price. Ask the salesman to justify his price by previous comparable homes that have sold in the recent past. After squeezing the price out of broker A, do the same with broker B and C. Their estimates of fair market value should be close. If you average the three, you have a fair market value.

Now that you know what your home is worth, you may proceed to offer it at a higher figure. Just how much higher depends on the custom in your local market. Your salesman should be asked for guidance on this matter. The reason for this is not only to give a buyer a "great deal" but to protect yourself in the event your buyer purchases with an FHA or VA mortgage. Remember, these types of mortgage require the seller to discount (pay points) his home as much as 9 percent. In this case, full asking price should be the only one you should accept.

Once the salesmen have given you the information you need, they may be dismissed. While dismissing a salesman is easy, getting rid of him is not so easy. If you've given yourself four months in which to sell your home and at least one month to try "by owner," then stick to your schedule. Respectfully ignore all salesmen's calls that 1) have located buyers who are willing to buy today or 2) who have changed their minds and decided your home is now worth more than they told you.

SHOWING YOUR HOME

Everyone lives with a certain amount of clutter in their homes. Everyone has a different "clutter tolerance," but even if your clutter is confined to the garage, attic or storage room, it's clutter nonetheless. It is important to remember that while everyone lives with clutter, no one buys clutter. This is the perfect time to have a garage sale. The last ten years have seen the garage sale come to full flower. I honestly believe that the American garage-sale gross national product exceeds the G.N.P. of any country that ends in a vowel.

You may start packing the day you place your home for sale. Clutter becomes respectable (and smaller) when packed in labeled boxes. Store the boxes in the attic, basement, a neighbor's house or at your new home, but never in the closets. All buyers have a closet fetish. Hang bikes, lawn mowers, garden tools, etc., from the joists or studs in your garage.

Selling and stowing your clutter not only improves the general appearance of your home but makes it seem larger.

This is also a good time to repair the minor house flaws we all live with. Cracked windows and plaster, loose tiles, leaking faucets, oil spots on the garage floor, minor settlement cracks in the foundation, unsightly lawns and water stains on the ceiling from an old roof leak can be easily repaired or hidden. These little visible things frighten the buyer as he suspects the worst of what is unseen. These little annoyances tend to blow up at negotiating time into major problems which are used to "justify" a ridiculously low buyer offer.

PROPERTY DATA SHEET

If you are listing your home with a broker, the property data sheet is handled by him and is an integral part of the listing agreement. However, if you're selling "by owner," it's a good idea to type and have copied the following information on your home.

Your local printer will run off the required number of copies at a nominal charge. When selling "by owner," data sheets not only

PICTURE OF HOME

Price:	$84,900
Address:	123 Elm St., Napco, Ill.
Tel. #:	AM: 123-4567 WK: 765-4321
Directions:	Main St. north to Arthur, east to Ash, south to Elm and east 2 blks. to home
Style:	Dutch Colonial
Exterior:	Brick and frame (aluminum-sided)
Age:	10 years
Lot Size:	80.2 × 140.6
Heat:	Gas-forced air (elec. baseboard, heat pump, etc.) humidifier
Floors:	Hardwood, carpeted, tile
Walls:	Dry wall (plaster)
Garage:	2-car attached, elec. door opener
Basement:	Full (½ plus 4' crawl) (crawl space) (none)
Tax 1978:	$1212.36
Reason for Sale:	Smaller (Relocating) (Transfer) (Liquidating)
Possession:	Oct. 15, 1980, or by agreement
Air Cond.:	Central air (Window units) (Heat pump)
Fireplace:	Family room, gas-started
Electric:	110, 220 (440)
Sewer:	City or septic tank
Gas:	Yes
Water:	City or well
Windows:	Thermopane (Stained Glass)
Schools:	Elementary Woodale 3 blocks
	Jr. high Bowen 6 blocks
	Sr. high Fenwick 3 miles, bus service
Transportation:	Commuter train 6 blocks (bus)

Rooms	Carpeted	Drapes	Dimensions	Level
Bdr.	Yes	No	15.0 × 11.2	2
Bdr.	Yes	Yes	12.3 × 11	2
Bdr.	Yes	Blinds	15 × 10.6	2
Bdr.	Yes	Yes	15 × 9.1	2
Fam. rm.	Tile	Yes	21.5 × 14.0	1
Liv. rm.	Yes	Yes	18 × 15	1
Din rm.	Yes	Yes	14.6 × 12.0	1
Kitchen	Tile	Yes	15 × 12.3	1
Bath	Tile	Yes	Full	1 & 2
Bath	Tile	Yes	½	1
Closets			Eight	

Additional Comments:

Immaculate custom-built, Dutch Colonial with formal entry. Kitchen features built-in dishwasher and self-cleaning double-oven range. Refrigerator negotiable. Water softener and electronic air filter included. Patio overlooks large professionally landscaped yard. Walk-in cedar closet in master bedroom. Owner will take dining-room chandelier and substitute. A great home for a growing family.—Call for appointment—

Information on this sheet is believed to be accurate but is not guaranteed.

provide information to the buyer but offer a ready reminder to the seller. The seller should be as complete and accurate as possible. As a precaution, the last sentence should always be included in order to protect against misunderstanding.

The picture of your home should be taken from an angle as this not only shows the length but the depth of your home and is in many other ways more complimentary.

Try not to include the color of anything on your data sheet or advertising. "Wall-to-wall custom carpeting" is good; "blue wall-to-wall custom carpeting" is bad. Any color you name will eliminate some percentage of readers. Buying is a chore and many buyers consciously or subconsciously look for excuses to limit homes on their itinerary.

Room sizes should be on the data sheet because the buyers think this is important. It's not. Most people have a hard time envisioning a 12 by 18 family room. Their judgment can be made only upon entering the room. Their judgment is subjective and instantaneous.

The principle advantage of a "by owner" seller is that he knows his home, its good points and bad, better than any salesman could possibly know it. Only he knows the civility of his neighbors, the sixth-grade teacher, utility bills, status of the heating system and a hundred other invisible features. If he accentuates the positive, a sale may be his.

Unfortunately, product knowledge is not everything. The intangible factor of neutrality which all real estate salesmen have is just as important. It is the nature of brokerage for the salesman to be neutral with regard to selling one particular buyer your particular home. The salesman is interested only in selling his buyer *someone's* home. His neutrality is a mood which is easily conveyed to the buyer in speech and behavior. Since the "by owner" seller is interested only in selling *his* home, he frequently sets a mood too intense for most buyers.

I have also found that, in terms of salesmanship, most sellers are equal to or better than most real estate salesmen and are frequently more enthusiastic. However, the advantage still lies with the salesmen as there are more of them. Should your listing be available to a thousand salesmen through a multiple-listing service, your chances of selling are greatly increased. Real estate is a numbers game.

And finally, due to the increasing complexity of financing, the real estate salesman has a more thorough knowledge of financing alternatives available to buyers.

As a "by owner" you may show your home to prospective buyers by an appointment made as a result of advertising or by having an open house. Open houses are generally held on weekends, and while it is a shotgun approach, it is more apt to attract the timid buyer. It has proven to be a very successful method of selling a home although it also attracts curious neighbors, antique buyers and unqualified buyers. It's difficult to qualify these buyers at the front door so you might as well welcome everyone and count the silverware when they leave.

Homes show best when they appeal to all five senses. For this reason, it is a good idea to have coffee available. It is never declined. It sets a friendly and informal atmosphere and usually requires the buyer to spend more time in your home. Background music also helps the ambience. Don't play the type of music that sets the hormones whistling but the type of tuneless tinkle you hear in a hospital elevator. Don't turn the television on as it might be tuned to something worthwhile and this can only distract.

Smell sells. Unfortunately the seller is least able to sense the ambient odor of his home. Smoking, pet or cooking odors are immediately sensed by the buyer. There are a number of commercial products on the market that can alleviate this problem. It is also a good time to swear off boiled cabbage.

One of the most common fears among sellers is the fear of burglary. Since the seller has no way of determining the intent of the open-house guest or appointment, he may naturally think that they are "casing" his home. This is more rumor than fact. While this may be true with upper-price-range homes, I know of no occurrence of this. Nevertheless, this fear is frequently played like a Steinway by many salesmen. It's an empty argument for them since they have no way of separating the wheat from the chaff. Can you imagine a salesman asking a buyer if he's a thief? Very few buyers enter a real estate office with nylon stockings over their heads. If you still feel uncomfortable with strangers looking through your home, your solution should be to store your valuables in a vault. If your items are too large, ask a friend, neighbor or relative to baby-sit them.

"By owner" sellers, in their enthusiasm, frequently forget to get the name, address and telephone number of potential buyers who have seen their home. A spiral booklet similar to the one you signed at your last wake is good but a legal pad will do. This list of names will be valuable to you should a change in the status (price reduction) of your home become necessary. It will also give you a list of buyer exceptions that can be included on a future listing agreement.

NEGOTIATING A CONTRACT

America has given three great ideas to the world: democracy, jazz and indoor plumbing. Bargaining is not one of them. This "art" is native only to those people who trace their ancestry to those countries bordering on the Mediterranean. However, the purchase of real estate and cars—the big-ticket items—require bargaining. It's expected and yet our previous experience does not equip us for this.

Real estate salesmen are better equipped to negotiate than sellers or buyers, not because they are different but because they are a neutral third party and therefore somewhat disinterested. If you're selling "by owner," you will increase your chances of success by having a friend or family member argue in your behalf with the buyer. A high asking price or a low buyer offer is more easily conveyed by a third party as it is not taken as a personal insult.

Since no one fires a starting gun to signal the beginning of buyer/seller negotiations, it is interesting to know not only when they begin but how to identify them. *Sellers and buyers begin negotiating upon first contact.* It could be at the front door during an open house or on the telephone as a result of an ad. At the front door a phrase such as "We were just passing through the neighborhood and . . ." The casualness of this opening statement is, consciously or unconsciously, both defensive and intimidating. Likewise, the seller's classic response is "Please come in and excuse the mess . . ." or, in other words, "You caught us unprepared." The signal both parties are trying to transmit is the uncivilized "I don't give a damn if this deal is consummated or not." This is negotiating.

Upon the buyer's inspection of the home, every opportunity is sought to find flaws. The degree of the buyer's subtlety in expressing his disapproval is only a direct measure of his manners and is still negotiating. Upon opening a closet, a barely audible "Tsk" by the wife is enough.

The seller should never lose his sense of humor with the buyer due to these signals. Anyone familiar with the mating dance of penguins would understand. It's a ritual. I've always suspected the buyer that loves everything about a seller's house. Since no negotiating signals are sent, the buyer is only looking for a graceful exit.

The best signal of all is "We're interested in the home but it's too much." An aware seller should immediately run to the closest pencil sharpener. This means "I want to make an offer on your home."

A second inspection by the buyer is another excellent signal even if it's preceded with "I'm trying to decide between your home and two others." The chances are the other two don't exist. The buyer is negotiating by trying to establish an auction environment.

BUYER'S NEGOTIATING STRATEGY

After you've decided to buy a particular property, your next step is to find out what the seller's lowest price is. Believe it or not, in most cases the seller isn't sure of this. How then do you find out the unknown?

Here's a good procedure to follow. Offer the seller a price he can't possibly agree to. If the seller is asking $71,900 offer him $63,000. Be careful. If the home is wildly overpriced, you may get it for $63,000 and still overpay. This shouldn't be a problem if you've done comparison shopping. Assuming the seller thinks you're serious, he will counter your offer at a price he feels his property is worth, say $68,000. The buyer now knows what the seller really wants. The $71,900 figure can be completely forgotten and $68,000 can now be used as a new base. The buyer can now accept $68,000, in which case he has bought the home, or volunteer to "split the difference." This brings the buyer's offer up to $65,500 from $63,000 and ideally the seller should drop from $68,000 to $65,500. This is a very successful final negotiating trick for the buyer. I suspect it owes its success to the fact that there is an aroma of fairness about it. Of course it cannot stand up to a very rigorous mathematical inspection.

CHOOSING AN ATTORNEY

Attorneys, like doctors, have become specialists. Therefore, it's best to select an attorney who concentrates on real estate since he can do the job more efficiently and cheaper. Your bank or savings institution may give you some help in selection as will your local real estate broker. Friends, family and neighbors are always willing to help with a recommendation.

The burden of closing a home lies principally with the seller. It is he who must provide all the necessary documentation. Therefore, all but the most sophisticated sellers need an attorney.

If the buyer is employing "creative financing," a land contract, if the seller is recently divorced, or when buying new construction, or if the buyer is just jittery, an attorney is necessary.

Attorneys' fees are governed in large part by their self-esteem. Once you've compiled a list of recommended real estate attorneys, ask them for their fees and select the most humble. Unlike a manslaughter rap, closing the average home is not that demanding; therefore, all can be considered equally competent.

Your attorney needs from you as a seller, your last tax bill, property survey, title policy and mortgage account number. If you've lost them, copies are available from your lender.

ADVERTISING YOUR HOME

No advertising can be effective without a profile of the typical buyer and an understanding of his motives. Only in this way can you fulfill Aldous Huxley's definition of advertising as "An organized effort to extend and intensify craving." There are three advertising media open to the seller:

1. Classified ad
2. "For Sale" sign
3. Word of mouth

Since successful advertising can best be measured by response and since the best response can be achieved only by maximum exposure, your wisest course is to employ all three.

Current national statistics show that the largest group of buyers are between the ages of 25 and 34, earn at least $15,000 and have three or more persons in the family. A Realtor Marketing Institute survey shows that buyers are interested in reading the following:

Information	Percent
(1) Location	67
(2) Price and terms	66
(3) Number of bedrooms	58
(4) Condition of property	55
(5) Convenience to schools	52
(6) Convenience to shopping	45
(7) Convenience to churches	45
(8) Number and size of closets	42
(9) Lot size	38
(10) Number of bathrooms	36
(11) Taxes	34

CLASSIFIED AD

Now that we know what the buyer wants included in the ad, let me recommend what you should tell him:

1. General location (not address)
2. Price
3. Number of bedrooms

4. Style
5. Best features

An ad that tells the buyer everything he wants to know about your home is not only expensive but counterproductive. Take your inspiration from the girlie photographer. His gauze-covered lens is forever shooting models playing the cello, facing the wrong direction or operating a wood lathe. An ad which gives the basics and just enough information to stimulate curiosity is ideal. You only waste time by playing peek-a-boo with the buyer on price as it is either (a) in or (b) out of his price range. The same is true of bedroom count, location and sometimes style as they may not suit the buyer's needs.

Special features may be defined as those aspects of your home that *you* most enjoyed. Every year tens of thousands of people buy fireplaces with attached homes, swimming pools encumbered by homes, wine cellars whose misfortune is to be located under a house or, most of all, quality schools that just happen to have your home as part of its constituency. Every home is unique and each has its advantages, even if it is only a low price. Special features make good headlines for your copy and should be stressed.

Take a tip from the politician and learn to master the art of meaningless words and phrases. Phrases such as "large country lot" could mean either 80 by 140 feet (which may be the largest lot in your neighborhood) or a parcel of land roughly the size of Nicaragua. "Spectacular family room" or (my favorite) "tastefully appointed" signify anything the buyer or seller want them to signify.

You will also do well to learn the political art of "misspeaking yourself." A tiny, cramped home is "cozy," a home three weeks from the wreckers ball is "rustic" and a home bordering on the B & O Line is "close to transportation."

Just as every home has its advantages so every home has its drawbacks. But, keep in mind, no buyer ever bought what he considered the perfect house. Everyone compromises. Also remember, no one ever bought a home solely on the basis of ad copy or made a commitment on the telephone. Sales can result only from a physical inspection. It is at this time that the buyer determines whether your home is too small, too large, or poorly situated, etc.

The only purpose of the classified ad is to make the phone ring, the only purpose of the phone ring is to set an inspection appointment and the only purpose of an inspection appointment is to sell. And remember, "The more you tell, the less you sell."

THE "FOR SALE" SIGN

The least expensive and most effective form of advertising for realtor or homeowner is, and always has been, the sign on the front lawn. Many buyers begin shopping for a home within a particular town or with a specific area in mind. Then, within these perimeters, they cruise. Should you get a "sign call," your chances are one out of five that the inquiry will result in a sale. The reason for this is that the buyer presold himself on many important characteristics of your home. He never would have called if he didn't like, or is willing to overlook, style, size, landscaping, exterior maintenance and, most important, location. He probably suspects that a well-maintained exterior is indicative of the interior, and, if he's an experienced house hunter, he has a good mental picture of the floor plan.

The "sign call" buyer, unlike the ad caller, is missing one important piece of information—*price.* If you can sell him your price, you have a sale.

WORD OF MOUTH

Gossip is probably the most overlooked of the sales media. Don't be afraid to tell all members of your family, neighbors, friends and everyone you meet about your intentions. This type of news can't wait to travel, and when it does, it does so on a one-to-one, conspiratorial basis. This type of advertising is more personal and therefore carries more weight than a classified ad or lawn sign. It may or may not work for you. If it doesn't, you can console yourself with the fact that it's free.

SELECTING A SALESMAN

On a national average, the "by owner" period lasts about two weeks. If you've given yourself enough time to sell your property, I recommend trying for at least a month. With a little more persistence, you might be successful. If you're not, then it's time to enlist the services of a brokerage firm. A good idea is to select the salesman who most impressed you when you were seeking an appraisal. Possibly his persistence in following up his listing presentation during your "by owner" period has impressed you.

No brokerage firm in your area has a monopoly on professionalism. Top salesmen can be found in large companies as well as small. If you're faced with a choice between a large company represented by a salesman of an unknown or doubtful professionalism and a small company represented by a salesman of known abilities and ethics, decide in favor of the salesman from the small company. Small companies with fewer listings will advertise your property more frequently. You may insist (get it in writing) upon signing the listing only if the broker guarantees weekly advertising. Don't forget to refer to your guest registry and list, on your listing agreement with your broker all those potential buyers of your "by owner" period as exceptions. Should any of these prospective buyers eventually buy your home, you do not owe a commission to the broker. Resist all the broker's attempts to limit the exception period to five or six days. Demand at least a month. If he wants your listing bad enough, he'll accept your terms. Dealing with your employee—your listing broker—is not a time for groveling.

Statistics show that 35 percent of the property owners in this country have a family member or close friend engaged in the real estate business. In many areas, this percentage is much higher. Avoiding your sister-in-law who entered real estate in order to "do something meaningful with her life" is a problem I can't answer. This sounds like a job for your family clergyman. Do the best you can to preserve your friend and family relationships as well as sell your home at the highest possible price in the shortest time with the minimum amount of fuss.

BUYING A HOME

For most people, buying a home is the largest expenditure they will ever make. For this reason, a thoughtful study is essential.

In most cases, the buyer has an idea of the general area in which he would like to live. This area may be large or small. It may be a county, city, subdivision or neighborhood. Confining your home search to your area not only eliminates confusion but in a short time allows you to become an area expert. Now that you have defined the perimeters of your area, you can forget the rest of the world. It only confuses.

It's now time to "cruise." Weekend afternoons are the best since you are more apt to inspect open houses. Bring along a pad of paper and make notes of:

1. Address and style of all homes for sale within your area. Including all "by owners" and those homes listed with a broker.

2. Schools, shopping, transportation, parks and distance to your work.

3. Open-house comments.

You should have a general "feel" for your area as a result of this cruising. Your next step should be to make appointments to see those "by owners" that interest you. At this point, you may think you understand the market. You don't. You never will until you've seen everything in your price range. At this time you'll need the services of a local real estate broker. Only he can show you listed properties in your area.

It's important to understand the motives of real estate salesmen. They only want to sell you a home. They know that the best way to do this is to show you the best buys currently on the market. A salesman gains nothing by trying to sell an overpriced listing. If your approach to the salesman includes the fact that you've previously inspected certain homes in the area, he will try even harder to get you the best possible home at the best price. An experienced salesman is also an invaluable source of area information and financing tips. You will also probably find that those "great deals" seen "by owner" are not so great after all. If you've seen twenty homes both on your own or with a salesman, at least one should stand out as the home for you. Buy it.

The decision to buy an older home or a newer home is one of personal taste. Both have their advantages. While an older home may have charm, mature trees, lower taxes, better construction and a more central and established location, it may also have an obsolete floor plan, be in need of repair or have a dated interior. Whether older or newer, there is a strong market for each.

You may also consider buying new construction direct from the builder. Builders frequently make prior arrangements for financing their units at terms unobtainable in current money markets. The disadvantage in buying new construction is that as much as $8,000 may have to be spent by the buyer in extras. A patio, wallpaper, storm doors, lawn and landscaping are just some of the grace notes overlooked when buying from the builder's plans.

THE TRANSFERRED BUYER

It's a well-known fact that our society in recent years has become increasingly mobile. Changing one's geography, whether imposed by an employer or by personal whim, is occupying an ever-increasing market share. The modern migrant is frequently bewildered by his new locale. To add to this problem, he is in most cases pressed to make a quicker housing decision. The local buyer, seeking to upgrade his home, not only has more market knowledge but has no such urgency.

In addition, coordinating the sale of the transferee's present home with the purchase of his new home is exaggerated by distance.

The real estate industry has adapted to this problem quite well. And for this reason I think the services of real estate brokers are essential.

Many real estate firms are either affiliated with national referral networks or, due to their national franchise characteristics, have their own built-in referral system. It is important that the transferee deal with a local broker who has the advantage of a national network.

The transferee is sent property data sheets of homes in his price range from a broker in his new area. While this is not a substitute for an actual physical inspection, it gives a good idea of prices, taxes and styles available, thus eliminating some original shock and confusion.

Some referral systems guarantee the sale of the transferee's home within a given period of time, thereby freeing the transferee to make a firm commitment in his new city.

Since most companies absorb the selling, moving, buying and temporary living costs of their employees, being transferred is economically preferable to upgrading.

In all cases, brokers treat the transferee as a preferred customer. As a buyer, he makes up his mind within a week, and as a seller, due to his company paying the commission, he is more pliant. Therefore, brokers tend to assign their most knowledgeable salesmen to the transferee. In addition, the transferee can expect the brokers to make transportation and hotel arrangements in his new city.

The transferee should first insist that his salesman give him a "Chamber of Commerce" tour of his new area. It is a characteristic of the transferred buyer that he buys a home and an area most comparable to the one he's leaving. It also requires a more concentrated effort. All housing decisions are the same as for the local buyer except, that for the transferee, they must be done in "quick march."

REHABILITATION

Restoring property for profit is an excellent investment. However, you must be able to do the remodeling yourself or know skilled and reliable people who can. It also requires more money than you may think. Area knowledge is also important and location is of prime importance. A dilapidated home in a dilapidated area is not a good rehab candidate but the same home in a good neighborhood is. Unlike buying your own home, you cannot afford to make a mistake and still rely on time and inflation to make you look smart. Arithmetic is important. This arithmetic not only includes an appraisal of the building when restored but may include estimates from contractors for a new roof, windows, doors, floors, siding, electrical, plumbing, landscaping, furnace and more. You must also consider your holding costs. Since acquisition and rehab costs are done with borrowed money, the quicker you can buy, fix up and sell, the higher your profit and the lesser the bank's. It's been my experience that these interim costs are the major expense in all rehab projects and the most overlooked. Banks are sometimes hesitant in lending money to rehabilitators without a proven history of building restoration. Since this type of loan entails some risk, banks may require you to play "You Bet Your House." This game requires you to put up your house or other properties you own as collateral. This is a test of your faith and the bank feels that if you're confident enough to bet your home then they are confident enough to lend you the money.

Not all run-down buildings are suitable for restoration. In many cases, the only solution is the wrecker's ball. However, if the building has a sound structure, a good or improvable floor plan, a character (charm) or the potential for character and a good location, it should be considered for rehabilitation.

It goes without saying that the sum of all this arithmetic must be less than the sale price of the restored property minus selling expenses. This difference is the profit.

This is simple in theory but increasingly difficult in execution. Since there is a strong market for the "handyman special," I have found that too many run-down properties are selling at prices which, when improvement costs are added, equal the selling price of the restored home. In many markets, finding the right property at the right price is the chief obstacle to success.

Maintaining a good relationship with various brokers is a help in finding this increasingly elusive type of property. Once you've found potential rehab property, it is time for the arithmetic. Cost estimates from your subcontractors, an appraisal from your broker of the sale price of the improved home and the financing costs based on an estimate of the time involved in fix-up and selling are your arithmetic. In addition, I advise, at least for the beginner, adding another 10 percent to satisfy Murphy's Law. In every project such as this, there are unforeseen problems.

Once you've found suitable property, the following should be considered:

1. If you have some experience in the field, buy your own building materials. Set up accounts with various building-supply houses—electrical, plumbing, lumber, hardware, etc.—their discounts to you may be as much as 50% less than retail and their catalogs are necessary for your arithmetic.

2. Act as your own general contractor and hire tradesmen to work directly for you. If at all possible, hire "moonlighters." Contracting directly with their employer involves an unnecessary expense.

3. It is essential that your employment contract with your subcontractors include that they:

(a) provide for their own insurance and income taxes,

(b) cart away their refuse,

(c) deliver on promised starting and completion dates.

Never pay the subcontractor in advance for his work, although you may consider an incremental payoff based on work progress. Paying for the entire job in advance frequently leads to tears, and tears are acceptable in life only if shed by someone else.

Decor is important in resale. Particular attention should be paid to the kitchen and baths. A little extra money spent here will be more than returned in a higher sale price. Since you're restoring the home in a short period of time, color and design coordination can be easily planned and implemented.

HOME ADDITIONS

A homeowner, satisfied with his neighborhood and schools but not with the size of his house, may move to a larger home or expand his present home. Rising prices and interest rates are making more and more homeowners opt for home additions. For this reason, home additions will become an increasingly more important factor in home ownership.

From an investment standpoint, the cost of an addition is not always recoverable upon resale. In too many cases an overambitious home addition either ruins the architectural appeal of the home or distorts an otherwise good floor plan.

A good thumb rule is to "keep it simple." The more complicated additions, including not only a family room but bedrooms, baths, enlarged kitchens, etc., generally yield a house oddity. I've seen finished products with second-floor living rooms, bedrooms whose only entrance is via another bedroom or kitchen, six-bedroom homes with one bath or structures that can best be described as family rooms with attached homes. Care must also be taken not to overimprove. While an improved home may cost $85,000 to reproduce, and if it is in a $50,000 area, realizing the full replacement price may be impossible. In addition, most home heating and, occasionally, electrical systems are designed to service a home no larger than the original square footage. An addition may exceed the design of these systems. This is not a serious problem but the addition of an auxiliary heating system is still an extra and, in many cases, unplanned cost.

For these reasons, I believe the services of an architect to be essential. He not only provides a set of prints acceptable to your local building department but saves a great deal of planning (time) by your subcontractors. He acts as a brake on your more bizarre and unworkable fantasies and he may present new and interesting ideas you may not have thought of. Architects' fees are generally a percentage (10 percent) of the job or they may charge an hourly fee. For a small project such as a family-room addition, it makes good sense to find an architect willing to work on an hourly basis (and don't bother him too much).

You may decide to have a general contractor supervise the work for you or you may short-circuit him and act as your own general contractor. While you save 15 to 20 percent by avoiding him, you don't have the advantage of a single guarantee, you inherit the organizational problems of the arrival of materials, the supervisory problems of labor, and, most of all, due to inexperience on your part, more time to completion.

Whether you play a direct role in your building addition or not, you have the advantage of stopping the work at your level of competence. Anyone can paint or hang wallpaper, many people can install dry wall or lay a tile floor, and some homeowners are capable of electrical or plumbing work. In all cases, some money is saved. The amount is determined by the extent of your skills.

The labor sequence is as follows:

1. Architect
2. Excavation and concrete work
3. Carpentry—framing crew
4. Roofing
5. Electrical and plumbing (heating)
6. Carpentry—interior finish (trim, floors, windows)

NEW HEATING CONCEPTS

Every age brings with it a new housing toy. Electricity, indoor plumbing, built-in appliances and, most recently, the first-floor family room, have all added to our life-style. We are currently witnessing a renewed interest in heating and heat conservation and the reason is obvious. Energy costs, which will continue to rise, are at an alarming rate. Since 1973, gas and oil have risen 83–113 percent and electricity by 50 percent. In the next decade, it is conservatively estimated that natural gas will increase 132 percent and oil and electricity by at least 70 percent. Government, the building industry and, most important, the buyers are becoming increasingly conscious of heating systems.

A savings of $30 per month in fuel costs translates to an additional $3,400 available for mortgage (based on a 30-year mortgage at 10 percent). To put it another way, a penny saved in heating costs for an individual earning $16,000 is 1.33 cents earned (before taxes), or saving $30 per month is equivalent to a $40 raise.

The true energy-efficient home will become a reality not through an improved social conscience but because it must. There is no other alternative. The President of the United States cannot make the homeowner dial down his thermostat to 68° but an Arab sheik can and will. You can save about 3 percent on your fuel costs for every degree you reduce the average temperature in your home.

The energy-efficient home of the future is not dependent on any one single technological breakthrough. The development of solar heating is a partial solution and I think one that will always be limited by geography. Improved insulation and weather stripping, more enlightened window placement and fewer windows, better energy-conscious design, more efficient heating systems will collectively add up to the ideal. I am convinced that a free economy and an increasing public awareness will put this energy stew together.

INSULATION

The performance of insulation is measured in terms of R values. The "R" stands for thermal resistance to heat flowing out in winter and flowing in during summer. The higher the R value, the better the resistance and performance of the insulation. When buying new construction, the smart buyer should insist upon the insulation requirements shown on page 133.

Since hot air rises, heat loss via the ceiling is the most important and therefore requires the highest R rating. If you have an unfinished attic, it is also the only feasible, major insulation improvement you can make in an existing home. Nearly all homes built prior to 1975 are underinsulated given current heating costs. It is estimated that 40 of the 70 million single-family homes in the United States are not adequately insulated. It's an easy do-it-

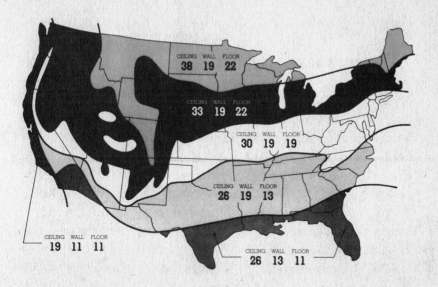

yourself project as it consists of little more than unrolling and cutting blankets of insulation to fit the joists.

Should your home sit on an unheated crawl space, additional heat conservation (and warm floors) can be achieved by stapling insulation blankets between joists. However, improving the insulation in your walls requires special equipment and the services of a professional and you may want to consider whether the cost and bother justify the savings.

Other heat-conservation measures you can make include:

1. Weather stripping of all doors and windows (a .5-inch crack under an outside door is like having an 18-square-inch hole in that door).

2. Caulking around door and window frames, outside faucets or electrical outlets or where chimney or brickwork meet siding.

3. Installation of double-glazed windows or storm windows.

4. Installation of storm doors.

HEAT PUMPS

There is nothing new about a heat pump. Its technology is at least 40 years old. It has been a standard heating and cooling system in the South for many years. However, in the last six years major design improvements (improved reliability) have made heat pumps economically feasible in more severe climates. It is now the most energy-efficient heating and cooling system commercially available in every state. Since it uses the sun's heat, it can then be said to be the only feasible solar heating system available. Due to the projected increasing cost of oil and gas relative to electricity, heat pumps' operating expenses will become even less for the remainder of the century.

Absolute zero or a complete absence of heat occurs at −460° F. Therefore, at 0°F. there is quite a lot of heat floating around. The heat pumps understand this. You don't. Using this principle, the heat pumps transfer heat from outdoors into your home in winter and from indoors out in summer. By simply reversing its operation, it is both a heater and air conditioner. The important point to keep in mind is that it takes less energy to move existing heat from one point to another than it does to produce heat. Most heat pumps can also easily accommodate gadgets such as electronic air filters, humidifiers, dehumidifiers and clock thermostats which automatically regulate your home temperature according to your needs.

Because a heat pump operates by absorbing heat from the outside air, there is a point at which it can no longer extract enough heat to fulfill your home's heating demand. At this point (balance point), generally around 30°F., electric supplemental heat or furnace heat (an integral part of the heat-pump system) begins to assist in the heating chores.

The good news about heat pumps is the 30 to 60 percent savings on your heating bill. The bad news is the high initial cost of the unit. A heat pump will cost $150 more per ton (a typical home has a two- to five-ton requirement) to install as opposed to other heating systems. Your local electric utility company will give you an estimate of your savings and, of course, your local heating contractor will give you the cost of installation.

As yet, the IRS does not allow a tax credit or deduction for this type of energy improvement.

GAS IGNITION CONTROL AND AUTOMATIC VENT DAMPERS

The pilot light on your gas heater burns unmolested in winter, summer or whether it's needed for ignition or not. When your heater shuts off, whatever hot air remaining in your heating system is vented through your flue into the outdoors.

A gas ignition-control device eliminates the constant burning of your pilot light and an automatic vent damper closes your furnace flue to stop the loss of hot air through the chimney whenever the burner is off. It opens just before the burner is lighted, thus conserving heat that is otherwise "burped" out. Both these devices are frequently installed as one package and your fuel savings may be as much as 20 percent.

You can recover the cost of these improvements in a relatively short period of time and since 15 percent of what you spend on this equipment is a tax credit, you are actually buying these improvements at a 15 percent discount.

ECONOMIC DECISION-MAKING ON ENERGY

All home heaters are able to maintain your home at the comfort level of 68–72 degrees but, like insulation and vent dampers, they do not delight the eye. Since their function is strictly utilitarian, your decision to install, repair, replace or improve should be a mathematical one. This is unlike buying a sofa, where personal taste plays a major role.

Industry frequently uses a pay-back schedule to make this type of decision. There is no reason why the homeowner shouldn't do the same. Let's take the heat pump as an example and let the following be true.

1. Your present, 25-year-old gas forced-air heater is beyond economic repair.

2. You have a choice of replacing it with another gas forced-air heater costing $1,500 or a heat pump costing $2,000.

3. The extra $500 investment in a heat pump can give you a return of 10 percent compounded as an alternative investment (utility bond).

4. The heat pump will save $20 per month on your heating-/cooling bill.

5. You will continue to live in your home for at least eight more years (the national average).

Since your $500 alternative investment will have grown to $1,070 in eight years and your $20-per-month savings on energy costs will, in eight years, equal ($20 × 12 × 8) $1,900, you are $850 richer. This simple pay-back formula ignores inflation or the fact that the price of natural gas is expected to increase by 130 percent within the next ten years.

If a solar-heating assist system can save you $50 per month on your heating bill and if the installation cost is $5,000 more than a gas forced-air heater, then $5,000 compounded over eight years equals $10,700. Then your fuel savings of ($50 × 12 × 8) $4,800 makes you poorer by $5,900.

You can get, free of charge, estimates of fuel savings on any system from your local utility or heat contractor. A simple thumb rule to follow is "the savings of fuel must equal, in today's dollars, the cost of the improvement within six years."

SOLAR HEAT

Solar heat is, at present, a parlor game for the environmenteers. The fact that solar heat is workable only within cannon shot of the equator is of no value to us or the equatorials. There is no technical basis to support the theory that solar panels will ever be able to supply the energy needs for a home at an affordable price.

A major, and as yet unthought of, breakthrough is possible and it will take nothing less than this to take solar heat out of the laboratory and into the marketplace. Stay tuned.

Windmill-generated energy is a fellow traveler of solar energy and suffers from the same defects. It's romantic, it's free, it excites the fancy, it has limited application and it is—well—quixotic.

SKYLIGHTS

Skylights are now being looked at for energy efficiency. They have a value as an energy saver but I believe that in addition to this, their chief value to the homeowner is aesthetic. I know of few other home improvements that add more to a home and its future sale price.

FIREPLACES

Most fireplaces are amusements not energy savers. Unless well-designed and glass-enclosed, they draw out more heat than they produce. In either case, they are aesthetically pleasing and minor (tolerable) polluters.

MOVING

No family activity is more chaotic than moving and few are more expensive. There is no way to make moving an experience in elegance but a great deal of confusion and uncertainty can be eliminated by understanding the procedure.

THE INTERSTATE MOVE

Large national carriers, when moving household goods across state lines, must charge rates determined by the Interstate Commerce Commission. This is primarily a function of weight and distance moved. Therefore it does no good to shop around for price. They are all the same. The distance between cities is fixed by ICC schedule and the total weight is determined by weighing the van before and after loading. The difference is the weight on which you pay charges. Should you suspect that the weightmaster might put his thumb on the scale, you can insist on being present at both weighings.

Without extra cost, your shipment is insured for $.60 per pound per article. This is rarely enough to cover your shipment. A commonly abused item such as a portable TV weighing 55 pounds when ravaged in transit will allow a maximum claim of only $33. You may therefore decide on additional coverage, in which case you will be charged $.50 per $100 of valuation. A good thumb rule to follow in evaluating your household goods is $1.50 per pound. The best proof of claim, and therefore the most painless way to collect on damaged or missing goods, is to note this at destination on the delivery receipt or inventory.

Other optional charges include cartons and professional packing and unpacking.

During the peak moving season, April through September, you should notify your mover one month prior to your moving date. During slower times, two weeks is sufficient. Shorter notice than this may prevent the mover from meeting your schedule. A mover's representative will, at this time, give you an estimate of your moving costs, but keep in mind this is only an estimate and not binding on the mover. The true cost of your move may vary 10 percent or more depending upon its actual not estimated weight.

Unless special credit arrangements are made in advance, the move is paid for at destination *before* unloading and the method of payment must be an irrevocable one such as cash, certified check or money order. Movers are realistic. In addition, the mover is not required to wait more than three hours at destination for you or your representative to accept delivery. If you're late, your furniture is put in storage and you pay for the privilege.

THE LOCAL MOVE

Moving rates within a state in excess of 50 miles are generally controlled by the individual state's commerce commission and under the same general terms as interstate moves. Local moves less then 50 miles are not controlled by any government authority. The cost of this type of move is generally computed on an hourly basis and may vary from $40 to $70 per hour. With this type of move it makes sense for you to shop for the most competitive price.

THE DO-IT-YOURSELF MOVE

If you are moving locally, have a strong back and are still speaking to your brother-in-law, a do-it-yourself move may be in order. By using a truck-rental agency, you may save 30 to 40 percent of your moving costs. Pads and dollies are also available at an additional charge, and finally, an ocean of experience indicates that the beer should be bought after your furniture is "in situ" at your new home.

The long-distance, do-it-yourself move is rarely worth the trouble. While you may save 12 percent, this is small compensation for the risks incurred due to inexpert packing and loading.

MONEY-SAVING MOVING TIPS

1. Before moving, discard as much of life's impedimenta as possible. Be merciless.

2. Have a garage sale.

3. Give items to charity and get a receipt of approximate value. It's deductible.

4. Collect all utility refunds (gas, electricity, water and telephone).

5. Collect from sellers all warranties and service manuals for built-in appliances.

6. Take valuables such as jewelry and important papers with you.

7. Ask your mover for a check list of things to do before moving such as giving a change of address for mail, newspapers, credit cards.

8. Keep records of all moving costs. Most are deductible.

INSURANCE

Insurance on your home is not an option, it's a necessity. If you have a mortgage, your lender insists on it. There are four categories of homeowner's insurance and each can be tailored to the homeowner's needs.

For most buyers, I recommend what is called "form three." This grade of insurance seems to offer the best balance between coverage and cost. If you don't like the cost of form three or any other grade of insurance, you can lower it by increasing your deductible.

Form three insures you against not only fire, lightning, theft and vandalism but anything else that can happen. It has been my experience that these "anything elses" generally happen. These include windstorms, hail, explosion, riot, aircraft damage, vehicle damage, smoke, ruptured steam pipe, roof damage caused by snow, freezing or accidental leakage or overflow of plumbing, and glass breakage.

It's a good idea to periodically review your policy to be sure that your coverage equals the increasing value of your home. Most policies automatically accelerate but this may not be enough.

Another type of insurance that may be of interest to the homeowner is "mortgage life." This type of policy is so structured as to pay off the mortgage in the event of the death of the breadwinner. This is reducing-term insurance and its only function is protection, not savings. Its benefits decrease at roughly the same rate as your mortgage. It also guarantees future insurability in whole life regardless of your future state of health.

CLOSING DOCUMENTS

The transfer of ownership takes place at closing or settlement and no evolution in real estate is more bewildering for both buyer and seller than closing procedure. It is for this reason that an attorney is essential.

There are eight documents common to most real estate closings.

The mortgage and mortgage note are of concern to buyer and lender and have been previously discussed.

1. Title Insurance Policy. This document, the cost of which depends on the value of the property and is generally shared by both buyer and seller, guarantees the buyer that the seller(s) is the true and sole owner of the property being conveyed. It also guarantees the buyer that there are no judgments or liens on the property other than certain exceptions listed on the policy. Should defects in the title subsequently be found, the title insurance company insures the owner against loss.

In several states, the Torrens System of title registration substitutes for title insurance. This type of guarantee is administered municipally rather than privately.

2. Warranty Deed. This document conveys property to the buyer and warrants that the seller(s):

(a) Has title to the property and the right to sell it.

(b) Transfers to the buyer a title which is good against third persons.

(c) Conveys property that is free of liens and encumbrances except those listed on the deed.

(d) Will deliver any other document that may be needed in order to make title good.

(e) If he cannot satisfy the above, will compensate the buyer for his loss.

A poor cousin of the warranty deed is the quitclaim deed. This is used when there is a suspicion that a third party such as an ex-wife might have an interest in the property being sold. It only conveys title, if any, and contains no warranty of title. It does not take the place of a warranty deed but only supplements it.

Deeds and title policies say about the same thing. There is, however, an important difference. A seller may subsequently become a mendicant or, worse yet, a corpse. How then is the buyer to be compensated? Answer: by the title company.

3. Bill of Sale. Just as a deed conveys real property, a bill of sale

conveys personal property. The sale of just about any improved parcel of real estate includes some personal property. Ranges, refrigerators, lawn mowers, etc., may be included in the contract sales price or charged for separately on the bill of sale.

4. Affidavit of Title. Since the closing takes place some days or weeks after the title search, an affidavit of title must be executed by the seller in order to guarantee good title in this interim. This sworn statement by the seller assures the buyer that since title examination no judgments, bankruptcies, divorces or unpaid-for repairs or improvements have been made.

5. Respa Form (Real Estate Settlement Procedure Act). This form discloses all costs to buyer and seller in the sale of improved real estate (one- to four-family)—and most important, all closing costs.

6. Survey. This document states the legal description of the property together with a drawing of the boundary lines, improvements, easements, and states whether there are any encroachments, violations of setback requirements or zoning ordinances.

Other documents may be included in a closing depending upon the nature of the real estate, financing circumstances or local custom (or law).

CHAPTER *8*

*P*ROPERTY MANAGEMENT

*Managing a ten-flat
is just like managing your home,
except ten times harder.*

—Author

*T*he difference between profit and loss in any real estate investment frequently depends upon skilled property management. Larger buildings, increasing complexity of maintenance and repair, the trend toward absentee ownership, the special management problems of condominium and town-house developments, the increasingly wistful attitude toward paying rent and the rise of consumerism have made property management a full-time profession.

A successful property manager must be thoroughly familiar with his market and competition. He must be familiar with advertising, insurance, salesmanship, accounting, repair and maintenance. The property manager must have the virtues of tact, patience, pleasantness, organization, authority, loyalty, honesty and, most of all, enthusiasm. When dealing with tenants, he cannot afford the luxury of trust, love or friendship. He cannot believe in such theological phlegm as "the essential decency of man." He must suspect everyone. He must suspect no one. On occasion, he may be required to break up a fight without getting himself drop-kicked in the heart. And finally, like all jobs which require constant public contact, he must be a trained or instinctive child psychologist. In short, he must possess all the character traits of a successful saloonkeeper.

Property management is a growth industry and the financial rewards are considerable. It's an excellent introduction to real estate for those without the means to be an investor. No college course can teach you how to be a professional property manager. It can best be learned by experience. Both part-time and full-time opportunities are available according to the size of the building.

The overwhelming advantages of real estate investment are widely known. Many professional people, while they have the investment capital necessary for a major real estate acquisition, do not have the time or stomach for management duties. This frequently results in their turning to more passive and less rewarding investments such as the stock or bond market. It is this type of situation that presents opportunities for the property manager.

As a property manager for an absentee owner, you are account-able to the owner but you enjoy a degree of autonomy not common in other lines of work.

For many reasons, women seem to have a natural flair for building management. In addition, as a live-in property manager, a woman is able to provide an income without leaving her home and its responsibilities.

Finding employment as a property manager is not too difficult. You may respond to a want ad or express your intentions to the owner of your building. However, I recommend that you register your name with all the real estate offices in your area and leave them a resumé. Many large realty firms have a property management department that not only offers employment but professional training. Small firms deal with many investors whose decision to buy investment property frequently hinges on the availability of diligent management.

Management fees vary according to area, the size of the building and the extent of the manager's responsibilities. The manager's salary may be a percent of gross income (5 percent is common), percent of net income, fixed fee with a commission on new rentals, fixed fee with a rent-free or reduced-rent apartment or fixed fee only.

The first step of management is the drawing up of a management agreement with the owner. This is nothing more than an employment contract, but like everything else pertaining to real estate, *it must be in writing.* Handshake agreements are useless in a society which has substituted litigation for honor.

This agreement should:

1. Precisely describe the property.
2. Precisely state the beginning and termination of the agreement.
3. Define the manager's responsibilities. These may include:
(a) Advertising.
(b) Securing tenants.

(c) Performing or supervising of repair and maintenance.

(d) Accounting and financial reporting.

(e) Rent collection.

(f) Responsibility for adequate insurance coverage.

4. Describe the limits of the manager's authority. This may include the authority to:

(a) Hire and fire employees.

(b) Determine rental rates.

(c) Authorize expenditures up to a certain amount without prior approval of the owner.

(d) Evict.

5. Report to the owner the status of the property, financial and physical, on a scheduled basis.

6. Manager's compensation.

7. State the intentions of the owner. Some owners want to maximize income while others want to increase the value of their investment by adding improvements.

Full occupancy is a goal of any investor. A $250 rental, if vacant for three months, translates to an annual $187.50 rental. In order to avoid "discounting" the units, an aggressive advertising and rental campaign is necessary.

In order to successfully "sell" your apartments to prospective tenants, the manager must know the competition, have a profile of his prospective tenants, know his building and thoroughly understand the features of his neighborhood.

Knowing the competition is easy. This information can best be gotten by reading their ad copy and posing as a prospective tenant. With this knowledge, a manager can easily price his units at market.

An understanding of local income levels, major employers, shopping centers, transportation, recreational areas, schools, churches, community services and points of interest is essential background knowledge for the manager. Only with this knowledge can the manager rent successfully and thereby sustain maximum occupancy. Advertising media open to the manager include the classified ad, lawn sign, brochures and mailings. And remember, the only function of real estate advertising is to create interest. Apartments are rented in the same way that homes are sold: upon physical inspection and one-to-one salesmanship.

VACANCY LEVEL

A high vacancy rate is not necessarily indicative of rents being too high. It may signify only inept management or correctable property defects. Likewise, a low vacancy rate does not necessarily indicate sound management. It could mean that rents are too low. In any case, the manager, upon taking over, should analyze his building. This can be accomplished by interviewing present and past tenants and by knowing the competition.

TENANT SELECTION

The most important management function may very well be the selection of tenants. A good group of tenants not only eliminates much of the aggravation of management but has a direct effect on the vacancy rate and net income. And yet, an eagerness to fill a vacancy frequently results in the manager accepting anyone who applies.

Once the prospective tenant has expressed a desire to rent an apartment, the first step is to ask him to fill out a credit application. The typical credit application includes:

1. Tenants' names, relationships, ages and occupations.
2. Present and previous employment of all working members of the family, including the addresses and telephone numbers of the employers and the periods of employment.
3. Present and previous residences, including managers' names and period of residence.
4. References: credit, checking and savings accounts, also include personal references.
5. Description of pets, if any.
6. Tenant's signature.

This credit application should then be submitted to the local credit bureau. You should get the results within five days. This charge varies, but $15 is about average and many managers require the tenant to absorb this cost. The credit history should not show any judgments, the tenant should not have a high amount of debt, he should be current on all charge accounts and he should not be a chronic slow payer. Of course, an indiscretion here and there is tolerable, particularly if the tenant can offer a valid explanation.

The credit report concerns itself solely with the tenant's past payment record. It has nothing to do with tenant behavior. In some cases, a financially responsible tenant may have a life-style not suited to your tenant profile. An inordinate devotion to pharmaceuticals, an obnoxious dog, bagpipe playing and frequent, loud party-giving may be some of his characteristics which would disturb the entire building. Being a troll is as important a reason to deny tenancy as being a financial deadbeat.

The best method the manager has of verifying the behavior of a prospective tenant is to call the landlord or manager of his previous residence (the apartment prior to the one he's currently living in). If he's a "lemon," his current landlord will give him a glowing report just to get rid of him, but the previous manager should level with you.

Every manager has a different idea of the ideal tenant. A manager who encourages the "swingles" tenant must be prepared to accept a certain amount of zaniness and (the good news) higher rent. The opposite is true of a building with elderly tenants. Once you've developed a tenant profile, stick to it.

As a management function, the importance of screening your tenants cannot be overstated. Refusing occupancy to an applicant may be difficult but giving occupancy to a "wrong note," sooner or later, becomes unbearable and expensive.

Financial and behavioral investigation may strike you as snooping. It is. However, life is an endless struggle to avoid being the victim and these biographies are essential to the process. All men are created equal and that's where it ends. Each man devotes the rest of his life to being unequal. The purpose of tenant selection is to choose only the most equal.

Declining a tenant is best done through the mail. The mail is a one-way and impersonal medium which doesn't require you to divulge the source or content of adverse information.

> Dear Mr. and Mrs. Doe:
> The information we have does not meet our requirements for tenancy at this time and we are returning your deposit check.

THE LEASE

The purpose of a lease is to set forth in clear and understandable terms the responsibilities of owner and tenant. A lease may be written, oral or implied, depending on the circumstances. The laws governing leases (also collections and eviction proceedings) vary from state to state. However, whenever possible, it is desirable to have a written lease. Most states require a written lease for a term of one year or more or for a guarantee of rent by a third party (co-signer).

A valid, written lease must show the following:

1. An owner/tenant relationship;
2. Signatures by both parties;
3. A description of the property, including street address and apartment number;
4. Amount of rent to be paid;
5. When rent is to be paid;
6. Period of time during which the lease is to be in effect.

The tenant is not required to give notice of vacating the premises upon the termination of a written lease but if he wishes to stay beyond the time, he must notify the owner (manager) at least two months prior to extending. This extension may be verbal, and his continued occupancy and the acceptance of rent by management constitutes an oral and implied lease. With this type of lease or any month-to-month lease, a thirty-day notice is generally required by one of the parties for valid termination. Week-to-week rentals require one week's notice.

At any time it is possible for a lease to be canceled by mutual agreement. If an owner sells his building, all of the leases remain in effect.

A smart manager should make sure his leases prohibit assigning or subletting without his consent. This allows management to retain control over the occupancy of the leased premises.

SECURITY DEPOSIT

Upon approving the tenant and signing the lease, the manager should collect a security deposit (generally equal to one month's rent). The function of the security deposit is to insure the owner against unreasonable damage during the tenant's occupancy. The manager should also collect the first month's rent in advance. Management should then have, on a $250 rental, $500 before giving the key to the tenant. The security deposit should be returned at the end of the lease period (it is not a substitute for the last month's rent) and only if there is no damage beyond normal wear and tear. This $500 collected up-front also gives management a cushion against slow payment and should be enough to sustain property income should eviction proceedings become necessary.

Many states require the building owner to give interest on security deposits. The amount and conditions under which interest must be paid vary from state to state and the manager/owner should familiarize himself with his own state law.

COLLECTING RENTS

Cheating the landlord out of rent is the world's oldest cottage industry. Uncollected rent may very well mean the difference between profit and loss on a building. The best way to avoid problems is to make a careful tenant selection, but despite even this precaution, problems do develop.

A firm and consistent collection plan should be established by the manager. Any "breaks" given to a slow-paying tenant are usually viewed by them not as an act of kindness but as moral weakness. This is no time for meekness. It's true that in the afterlife the meek shall inherit the earth, but in the meantime they'll get it shoved up every conceivable aperture.

The antiquity and sophistication of rent-evasion schemes have stimulated an equally ancient and sophisticated body of law used to protect the rights of both tenant and landlord.

RENT COLLECTION

In order to avoid problems (legal and social), the law of the state in which the building is located should be followed at all times.

If a tenant's rent is due on the first of the month and if on the fifth, despite a courteous reminder by the manager, the rent is not received, then a suit for possession may be started. The law requires the manager to serve notice to the tenant before beginning the suit. In most states, a five- or ten-day notice is required before filing a suit for possession based on a default in payment under the terms of the lease.

In most cases the pinning on the door of a five-day notice is enough to get all or at least part of the rent from the blackguard. If, however, it goes to court and the judge awards a judgment for possession to the landlord, the tenant must peaceably leave the premises with his belongings in tow.

In all disputes with tenants, it is essential to follow the law. To do otherwise is not only ineffective but it may get *you* in trouble with the law. Threats, curses and provocative gestures with a chain saw rarely collect the rent and in all cases disturb building serenity. If renting an apartment requires the charm of a heavily tipped French waiter, collecting overdue rent requires the exactitude of a German policeman enforcing jaywalking. This is nothing more than constructive schizophrenia.

Countless situations develop in property management which require improvisation and common sense. For example, a tenant who cannot meet his rental payment on the first but who can on the tenth, upon the receipt of his commission check, may be given extra time. This, of course, could be a ruse, but since you have a security deposit and his rent is paid in advance, you have some security. Well, you can let go of a few drops of the milk of human kindness, but never do this unless you present it as something more magnanimous than the Marshall Plan.

RIGHTS OF THE TENANT

Tenants have the right of quiet enjoyment. However, a clause should be inserted in the lease which allows the owner or manager entry at reasonable hours for inspection, repair or showing the property to prospective tenants, buyers or appraisers.

A tenant may abandon the property if the landlord allows the premises to become uninhabitable. This could occur due to the landlord's failure to repair a defective heating plant or the removal of the front door, etc. Should this happen, the tenant may be entitled to recover damages.

DECORATING AND MAINTENANCE

A well-maintained and -decorated building yields higher rents, happier tenants, full occupancy and a minimum amount of tenant turnover. Maintenance is made easy by the implementation of an ongoing preventive maintenance program. As part of this program, periodic inspection of the building should be undertaken. Every unit in an apartment building should be inspected at least once every six months. Some tenants are lax in reporting problems and this could result in serious damage. Records should be kept of all repairs and replacements.

The total cost of maintenance breaks down to 10 percent for parts and 90 percent for labor! This should surprise anyone not experienced in apartment ownership or management. For this reason, owners of smaller apartment buildings seek out a neighborhood handyman. He is frequently a retiree and can be employed on a part-time or when-needed basis. He has a familiarity with electrical systems, appliances, plumbing and carpentry. While a major repair such as a new roof is beyond his ability, the day-to-day repair and maintenance items are not. Upon buying any building, the buyer should get from the seller the names of those used for these repair and maintenance services.

Every equipment manufacturer includes a service manual for installation, operation and service. Implementing the service instructions in these manuals will prolong the life of the equipment through a regular service schedule. In addition, parts are ordered by model and serial number and much time (and an expensive service call) can be saved by ordering parts through the manual.

The manager should record all tenant requests for service in writing. Promptness in handling these requests is important. An original and one copy of all requests should be made. The original should be kept by the manager and the copy should be used as a work order. The work order is then signed and dated by the person completing the job and returned to the manager. A file of maintenance and repair requests not only helps the manager monitor expenses but helps in making replacement decisions.

An apartment is generally cleaned between occupancies. Apartment cleaning is often done on a contract basis. It is important that the manager and the cleaning contractor have the same idea of the definition of clean. A problem-free and satisfactory job can be expected only with a clear, up-front and written understanding.

Choice of colors is important in any apartment. Correct color choice can brighten a dark room, make a small room spacious, coordinate seemingly unrelated objects or give intimacy to a large room.

Before painting, surfaces should be clean and free of old paint scales. The best quality paint should be used. Good paint will look better, clean easier and last longer. And keep in mind, labor, not material, is the most important consideration in maintenance.

The choice of a professional paint contractor is recommended over an unknown amateur. A professional may charge more but there will also be a savings in less time and material used and his job will always be neater.

Apartment carpeting should be long-lasting, stain-resistant and static-free. Currently, the best carpeting to buy for the money is a heat-twisted, low-profile nylon. This type of carpeting is available under many trade names and costs about $9.00 per square yard (installed). The manager, upon installation, should save all extra carpet pieces. These can be used for future patchwork.

Draperies, like carpeting, should be neutral and patternless. This will resist sun-fading and will blend with any tenant's furnishing.

Major repairs such as a new roof or heating system are generally contracted out. Cost estimates should be submitted in writing on a bid basis. The lowest bid is not necessarily the best choice. The reputation and experience of the company must be taken into consideration.

INSURANCE

An apartment building must have an "all risk" policy covering all physical damage to the building and contents. An apartment owner should also have liability protection to protect against injury to anyone within the building. Liability protection may also include personal injury in addition to bodily injury. These personal injury items include: invasion of privacy, slander or wrongful eviction or entry. A $1 million liability protection is recommended; however, a lower amount is available at only slightly less cost.

Protection against loss of rental income during the restoration of a damaged building may also be part of the insurance package. All of these risks, including protection against employee dishonesty, may be insured under what is called a package policy. The advantage of buying a package policy is that you get a discount of about 20 percent on your premium.

"Workman's compensation" is not included with a package policy. However, since most building owners employ labor, even if it is only on a casual basis such as snow removal, workman's compensation is almost always necessary.

CONDOMINIUM MANAGEMENT

As condominiums grow in popularity, so does the demand for skilled full-time managers. The manager or management firm is generally paid on a per-unit basis out of the monthly owner assessment. Unlike the apartment manager, the condo manager is not the boss of bosses. He works for an elected board of condo owners. Members of the board are frequently elected for their ability to yell and not for their expertise or understanding of the supervisory nature of their job. In addition, boards are elected every year and the "outs" like to portray the manager as a well poisoner in order to achieve victory.

Being a condo manager, while it generally pays well, is also a rather turbulent line of work. I suspect that as condo ownership becomes more widespread, education in condo living by board members, managers and owners will bring a greater efficiency to management.

The duties of the condo manager include the:

1. Preparation and administration of the budget. This budget must be approved by the board of directors.

2. Collection of the condominium assessments. In the event that assessments cannot be collected from a particular owner, most states allow the condo association to put a lien on the delinquent property.

3. Keeping of books, records and monthly financial reports.

4. Responsibility for the annual or semiannual report to the board.

5. Enforcement of the condominium regulations.

6. Supervision of all maintenance and repairs.

In performing these duties, a condo manager should always remember that he is responsible to the unit owners *through the board of directors.* Special favors performed for individual members sooner or later create dissension throughout the building. For this reason, it is absolutely essential that the manager perform his duties "by the book."

RENT CONTROLS

Rent control is a legal maximum on rental price. There are many variations on the theme and all trace their roots to World War II. It was then thought that rent controls would end once the Hun was rebridled. New York, however, tended the flame. During the seventies, four more states and the District of Columbia authorized some form of rent-control regulation. Due to inflation, there is now, in many areas, agitation for an expansion of rent controls.

Few things in real estate are sillier and none are more damaging to the tenant and ultimately to the community than rent controls.

The owners of apartment buildings, when faced with an artificial lid on rents, have two alternatives to follow in order to sustain their investments. They may convert to condominium or "milk" the building by skimping on repairs and maintenance.

Mass conversions further reduce the number of apartment units in the community, which results in an upward pressure on rents in other buildings.

The alternative of "milking" the building is more obvious to the tenants. In the long term, this results in a government-created slum with the final stage being a wasteful building abandonment.

Mortgage lenders do not like to lend on rent-controlled buildings and, if they do, the higher risk involved forces them to charge a higher interest rate. This is a further upward pressure on rents.

In addition, the decreasing value of rent-controlled apartment buildings and the high percentage of tax delinquencies tend to shift the tax burden to the local homeowner.

This system is almost perfect in that it hurts almost everyone: apartment owner, single-family homeowner, tenant and most of all the community. It does not hurt the vote-buying, populist politician and a number of upper-middle-class schemers who are accustomed to rent-controlled housing and use the poor as a Trojan horse to gain for themselves a free lunch.

SUMMARY

This chapter may impress you as being unreasonably cynical. It's not. Only by understanding certain mathematic and social brutalities can one approach the management ideal of a building that runs itself. As for being cynical, no one ever lost money by being so.

Whether you manage your own property or manage for others, the same principles apply: enlightened tenant selection, units priced at market, prompt attention to maintenance and repair and a courteous, firm, legal and universally applied method of rent collection.

Proper management also sustains building value. I have seen many apartment buildings sell below market solely because of leisurely management. This type of situation presents opportunities for the investor who is willing to "clean house."

Apartment-building management was discussed but this is not the only opportunity for property managers. If it's real estate it can be managed. Commercial, industrial and single-family residential are other avenues open to the manager.

No book could explain all the day-to-day situations that confront the property manager. It is for this reason that management requires endless improvisation and the full use of horse sense.

There are two national trade associations that are helpful to property managers. The Institute of Real Estate Management and the Building Owners and Managers Association. Membership in these organizations not only allows the property manager to gain valuable professional knowledge but helps him to keep current on new trends in the industry.

CHAPTER 9

SYNDICATION

*A partnership never thrives unless ingrafted
upon a stock of known and reciprocal merit.*

—Lord Chesterfield

*T*he word "syndicate" is a general term used to describe any association formed for the purpose of transacting business. It may take the form of a partnership, corporation, joint venture or trust together with all their variations. The type of organization depends upon the investment and the investor's objectives. However, three important considerations must be made:

1. Personal Liability. Can the investor(s) be held responsible for an amount greater than his investment? In other words, will the organization provide limited liability to the investor?

2. Tax Consequences. How will the organization's tax rules affect the individual investor?

3. Effect of Death or Divorce. How will the death or divorce of one of the investors affect the title and marketability of the property?

Syndications are becoming more popular as the cost of real estate escalates. In many cases, only through a collective approach can enough investment capital and expertise be assembled to handle a deal. Land development, shopping centers, apartment complexes and condominium conversions are typically made possible through syndication.

There are three reasons for taking on a partnership: money, talent or work. Hand-holding or companionship is not one of them. A good rule to follow is "do it yourself." But since this is not always possible or advisable, then what should partners look for in each other?

The financial partner (angel) should ask himself whether his working partner has the expertise. What is his track record? Can he be trusted?

The working partner should ask himself, "Can my angel provide enough money and easily enough to make a success of the undertaking and will he see it through even if things get rough? Does my angel know how real estate investments 'work'? Is he decisive? How long will it take to get a binding decision out of him?"

No syndication agreement, no matter how well written, can foresee every conceivable problem or contingency. For this reason, friendship and/or at least compatibility and trust are the bonds of any collective effort. Any written agreement is nothing more than an attorney's best attempt to keep the peace.

TENANTS IN COMMON

This form of co-ownership, unless stated otherwise in the deed, is assumed when two or more people, not married to each other, take title to property. The deed can state the fractional interest each owner has and if no fraction is stated then two owners are assumed to have one-half interest each; three owners, one-third interest, etc. In case of the death of one of the owners, his interest in the property goes to his heir(s), not his co-owner(s), although he (they) may be one and the same. Therefore, the death of an owner may affect the marketability in the transition period following death. Also, investors do not have limited liability—other personal assets are unprotected, not just the original investment. In addition, this type of direct ownership allows the income tax benefits to flow through directly to the co-owners.

A co-owner can sell his portion of the property without the consent of his co-owners.

JOINT TENANCY

Another type of co-ownership is joint tenancy. Unlike tenancy in common, should one of the co-owners die, his interest in the property passes to the surviving co-owner(s) and without the necessity of probate proceedings. This is the common form of home ownership. Also many investors do not want to have their share of an investment pass to unrelated investors. Tax and liability considerations are the same as with tenancy in common.

JOINT VENTURE AGREEMENT

The joint venture is another collective approach to investment. The joint venture agreement can be written any way the investors see fit, but the following procedure is typical.

Let's assume that partner A has the talent necessary to bring a land-development endeavor to a successful conclusion and partner B has the money to finance it. This typical money/expertise trade-off has a 50–50 relationship between the partners although I see nothing sacred about this ratio. Usually, the angel receives all the cash flow until he has recovered 100 percent of his investment. The remaining cash flow is then split evenly between the two. The angel's original investment may or may not bear interest. This depends upon the wording of the agreement. In many cases the angel will insist on some money contribution from the working partner. This gives him an additional sense of security in that some financial penalty is imposed should the project not be brought to a successful conclusion.

This type of syndication allows tax benefits to flow through to the individual investors and is not usually affected by the death of an investor. (This depends upon how the agreement is written.) There is also no limit on liability of the investors.

The general partnership and the joint venture can be treated the same except that a joint venture agreement concerns itself with one particular objective (i.e., the development of one particular parcel of land rather than any investment activity that happens to come along).

LIMITED PARTNERSHIP

The limited partnership is probably the most popular form of syndication. The limited partners have flow-through tax benefits, title is not affected by death and the limited partners have limited liability. However, the general partner within a limited partnership usually has unlimited liability. There are situations in which a partnership is treated for tax purposes as a corporation. The rules are quite complex, and if any doubt exists, the advice of an accountant should be sought.

CORPORATION

A corporation is made up of a group of persons granted a charter legally recognizing them as a separate entity having its own rights, privileges and liabilities distinct from those of its members.

The average investor is interested in what is called a subchapter S corporation. There are other varieties but they are of interest only to larger investors. A subchapter S corporation has limited liability, is not affected by the death of a shareholder and has flow-through tax benefits just as in a partnership. However, if the corporation has more than ten shareholders, it will not qualify for a partnership type of tax treatment. This type of corporation can also be denied partnership tax treatment if more than 20 percent of its income is derived from passive sources such as rent or interest.

A member of a corporation has the advantage of raising money by selling all or part of his shares without affecting the property or the structure of the corporation.

SUMMARY

An attorney, and, in some cases, an accountant, must be consulted before choosing a syndication form. The attorney will draw up the necessary documents, but remember his best efforts are no substitute for a "working relationship among the partners."

Syndication is becoming more important as the scale of real estate increases. It is the springboard from which the average investor can leap into intermediate and large investments. To put it another way, $300,000 is not a lot of money if approached collectively.

In many cases, banks and savings and loan associations are becoming bored with taking their profits in interest only. They are now good places to start for the investor looking for a money partner.

CHAPTER 10

CONDOMINIUM CONVERSION

Man alone aspires to be both in one, a social solitary.
—J. Bronowski

*T*he condominium concept of ownership dates from Roman times and has since enjoyed wide popularity in Europe. An example of this popularity can be seen in postwar Paris, where over 90 percent of residential housing starts have been condominium units. After having considerable success in South America, this concept came to us in the early sixties. While the growth of condominiums throughout the sixties was excellent, the seventies have demonstrated a skyrocketing popularity beyond everyone's predictions. I believe it to be the greatest single real estate phenomenon since the Homestead Act. Furthermore, it is modestly predicted that within fifteen years half of our population will be living in condominiums. We are currently living in condominium boom times and anyone who jumps in now can be said to be getting in on the ground floor.

It is, however, worth recalling that the years 1974–75 were (for the economy in general and condos in particular) awful. It is important for the investor to know not only the market factors responsible for the current boom but those responsible for the '74–'75 bust.

WHAT WENT WRONG

In 1974 we witnessed the worst recession since the thirties. The energy crises and excessively high interst rates (in most cases higher than state usury limits) combined to damage the entire real estate market. Condo developers, however, having benefited from the fat years ('70–'73), failed to pull in their horns soon enough. In short, they overbuilt. The resort condos were particularly hard hit as their purchase is discretionary and the spending of this "mad" money is the first thing to go in hard times.

Secondly, the high profitability of condo development in the '70–'73 period attracted inexperienced and sometimes unscrupulous developers into the business. Poorly designed and marketed developments led to lack of sales and resulting bankruptcies.

And, finally, the news media picked up on condominium abuses. Their indignation was soon transmitted to various other causemongers and before long congressmen and bureaucrats went on "full toot." Before any silly laws were enacted, concerned and responsible members of the condo industry begged Congress to disregard the news and find out the facts. They did and their findings showed that 1) 95 percent of condo owners were completely satisfied with their units and 2) nearly all condo abuses were limited to Florida. This survey not only took Congress off the warpath but allowed for an unemotional inquiry into those abuses. Among the complaints of dissatisfied condo owners were:

1. Questionable sale techniques
2. Inadequate notice to tenants by condominium converters
3. Low estimates of common expenses
4. Poor construction
5. Expensive and unprofessional management

A solution to these problems has been effected on a state and local level. Every state and many municipalities have condominium acts or ordinances.

Anything new, complex and immediately successful as condominiums is bound to go through a period of growing pains and the years '74–'75 were it. The year 1976 saw the beginning of an upturn which I feel is permanent.

CONDOMINIUM VS. CO-OPERATIVE

There are two types of multiple ownership of real estate, the condominium and the co-operative. The difference between the two is legal not physical.

As a condominium owner, you own your individual unit plus a pro rata share of the common elements (i.e., swimming pool, tennis courts, etc.) and you are individually responsible for paying your own mortgage and taxes. Under the co-operative form of ownership, you are a shareholder and given a proprietary lease in your unit. The corporation is subject to one mortgage and one tax bill. The disadvantage of this form of ownership is that if any member of the co-operative defaults on his share of the mortgage payment or taxes, the other members must make up the difference.

The preferred form of ownership is therefore the condominium. The only area of the country where co-operatives have enjoyed popularity is New York City and even this is changing. I predict the future of co-operatives to be no greater than 3-D movies.

ADVANTAGES AND DISADVANTAGES OF CONDOMINIUM OWNERSHIP

The typical condo buyer buys something more than real estate,* he buys a life-style. This life-style includes a freedom from most maintenance cares, the access to otherwise unaffordable amenities such as saunas, tennis courts and swimming pool, a security from the ambient condition of our cities—mayhem—and, above all, location. In addition, the condo buyer also enjoys all of the economic advantages of single-family home ownership such as equity payoff, appreciation and tax deductions. Briefly stated, the condominium owner enjoys the best of both worlds. He reaps the economic advantages of home ownership and the convenience of renting.

The disadvantages of condo ownership include smaller unit size, 1,250 square feet *vs.* 1,750 for single-family housing, and higher population density. These objections, however, are becoming less important as life-styles change.

WHO BUYS CONDOMINIUMS

The typical condo buyer has been an empty nester or, as some poet phrased it, "the newly wed or nearly dead." Retirees, young couples, swingles or high-income families looking for vacation property have, in the past, sustained the condo market. A survey revealed that the typical condo buyer was either over 55 or under 35 and more than half had previously owned a home. The median income of those polled was $24,900—considerably more than the national average. However, recent studies are pointing to a more

*Properly speaking, air rights.

universal acceptance of this concept. I can envision, in the not too distant future, a day when the typical city dweller's every contact with real estate will be with a condominium. He will reside, work, shop and vacation in them. Condominiums currently represent close to 50 percent of the for-sale market in Southern California, Chicago, Washington, D.C., and over half the market in southern Florida and San Francisco. While resort and residential condos are well known to us, commercial and industrial condos have yet to make their predicted impact. I suspect it's only a matter of time before the retail and service industries overcome their timidity and jump, headfirst, into this ownership concept. The advantage to the small businessman is enormous, as it now may be the only way he can afford to own a central business location.

CONVERTING THE APARTMENT BUILDING INTO A CONDOMINIUM

The condominium converter's profit is based on the principal of the sum of the parts being worth more than the whole. For example, a six-unit apartment building bought at $20,000 per unit ($120,000) and improved at $10,000 per unit ($60,000) equals a total investment of $180,000. The units when sold individually at $48,900 yield a total sale price of $293,400. The converter then shows a gross profit of $113,400.

Conversion is enormously popular with small investors due to the minimum amount of construction expertise required. The converter is essentially a refurbisher rather than a builder.

This type of investment is also somewhat blunderproof. Should the converter be unable to sell his units or should the state or municipality obstruct or make unfeasible the conversion plans, he still has income property. If he bought the building at the right price and terms, he should do quite well as a landlord.

Condominiums are a more economical use of increasingly scarce prime land in and around major metropolitan areas. It is this feature of central location along with an older building's quality of construction that will continue to sustain the condo conversion market.

SELECTING THE BUILDING

There are three important factors to consider when buying real estate: (1) location, (2) location and (3) location. However, when buying a building for conversion, there are four: (1) location, (2) location, (3) location and, most of all, (4) location. Every city has an area so desirable that land costs eliminate the feasibility of single-family construction. In these areas, the condominium is the only residential housing available to middle- and in some cases, upper-income buyers. It is in these areas that apartment conversion has the best chance of success. In smaller towns or suburbs, quality residential neighborhoods, close to transportation, also offer an excellent opportunity for conversion. It is of prime importance that the converter understand the surrounding area of a prospective conversion. Previous successful conversions within the area are a good indication of future success. Average household income is also important.

The age and condition of a building also determine its convertibility. All states now have condominium acts and many municipalities amend these acts with local ordinances. Their function is not only to ensure that the buyer is purchasing a sound building but to protect the rights of the tenants who may be displaced. In some areas, the day is long past when painting, a few evergreens and various other cosmetic changes are sufficient to fool the buyer or local building inspector. A converted apartment building may now have to be restored to a like-new condition in order to be marketed. These laws can only help the industry by ensuring the buyer of a sound investment and eliminating the amateurs and reprobates from this field. Oh yes, it also justifies higher prices. Extensive repairs to the building's systems (heat, plumbing, electric, etc.) or shell (foundation, walls, roof) may make its restoration too costly for consideration.

Before buying an apartment building suitable for conversion, the converter should check the tenant history of the building. Ask the seller for a copy of all leases. A high vacancy rate or turnover may indicate serious problems either in the structure or surrounding area. It may, however, indicate only a plantation approach to property management by the current owner. In this case, a building with a poor history may still make a successful conversion. Experience has shown that a successful apartment building invariably becomes a successful condominium. It is also important to remember that the average condo buyer insists on more square footage and a better view than the renter. Spacious units with large bedrooms and kitchens along with a postcard view are guarantees of success.

First-time converters should play it safe and select a small apartment building with deluxe units and preferably in an area of proven conversion success. Zoning should not be a problem as zoning concerns itself with density rather than form of ownership and a condominium will have the same density as the apartment building.

Before purchasing the building, the converter should become thoroughly familiar with his state and, in some cases, local condominium laws. Some ordinances are so strict as to effectively prohibit conversion. An attorney specializing in condo conversion is essential at this point. I also suggest, if you're not thoroughly familiar with the market, that you hire an appraiser to estimate the converted unit sale price. If possible, the converter should also protect himself by paying no more for the building than its value as an apartment building (use one of the income approaches to value).

It is also necessary to get an engineering report in order to determine the condition of the structure. The plumbing, electrical and mechanical components, heating plant, roof and other structural elements are inspected by a structural engineer in order to estimate the remaining useful life of these components. In this report, replacement and repair recommendations are made and, depending on local requirements, these recommendations may have to be implemented.

In many cases, the owner of an apartment building may wish to convert his building in order to realize a higher sale price. The owner's conversion point may be reached when he no longer reaps his desired depreciation deduction. However, it should be remembered that an apartment owner who converts and sells is considered a dealer and therefore loses his capital gains status.

In some marketing areas, an apartment owner who wishes to avoid the problems involved in conversion may, for a percentage fee, employ a firm specializing in conversions to do this work for him.

Here are two thumb rules that will assist you in making an instant analysis of any building, and remember, a thumb rule is no substitute for a thorough investigation.

1. A condo unit should be priced at 70 percent of the single-family homes of equal square footage in the same market.

2. The converter's profit should be at least 20 percent of the value as an apartment building in order to compensate for the risk, time and effort involved.

Purchase price of a 6-unit apartment	$150,000
Minimum expected return ($150,000 × 20%) $30,000	
Total costs of conversion @ $12,000 per unit	72,000
Total investment	$222,000
Average selling price of a single-family home in the area is $60,000	
Projected sale price of condo units	
$60,000 × 70% = $42,000	
Building gross (6 × $42,000)	$252,000
Profit to converter	$30,000

Once you've selected a sound building with a good tenant history in a desirable neighborhood, it's time to estimate conversion costs. Estimates from carpenters, electricians, plumbers, roofers, appliance dealers, etc., will give you the cost of the physical improvements. Attorneys' and surveying fees are the principal legal costs. Other costs that are easily overlooked by the inexperienced converter are sales costs, loss of rental income during renovations and, most of all, the interest expense on the construction loan.

Once you know all of your conversion costs, you're ready to see the banker. These loans are somewhat difficult to get for a first-time converter. However, if you've done your homework and are willing to pledge your own home as collateral, the loan can be yours. Lenders have a good reason to be selective with this type of loan as they remember the bad years of '74–'75 and are in no hurry to take another "bath."

You will be asking for at least two loans:

(1) a mortgage loan on the building with, say, a 30 percent down payment and (2) a construction loan for the costs of conversion.

No down payment is required on a construction loan and the interest, say 14 percent, is charged only on that amount of money you have withdrawn from your loan account at any stage of development.

Time is money, and due to the cost of money, speed of conversion is essential. If two similar buildings were converted and sold in 12 months and 18 months respectively, much of the converter's profit would be lost in the longer conversion.

Once you've signed a sales contract for the building and your mortgage and construction loan have been approved by the bank you may notify the building tenants of your plans to convert. State and city laws vary regarding the length of notice the converter is required to give—from three to 18 months.

It's a good idea to notify all tenants on the same day by registered mail, and don't forget to include a sales pitch. A successful converter I know has a policy of taking the tenants out to dinner where he announces his plans and answers any questions.

A clear, frank and complete discussion of the conversion plans are necessary in order to combat rumor. Allowing gossip to work its way around the building inevitably leads to trouble. The nursery rhyme "Chicken Little" was written for the converter. By the time a conversion rumor reaches Foxy Loxy, the sky really is falling.

Since the costs of condo ownership may exceed the rent by 15 percent, a sales presentation to the tenants should emphasize the tax and emotional advantages of ownership as opposed to renting.

If one third of the tenants sign a purchase agreement, this is a guarantee of the future success of the conversion. It is common practice to offer the tenants a discount for purchasing their own units. In many cases they have been responsible for the decor of their apartments and do not want the improvements of the converter. This is a savings for you.

The difference between a condominium and an apartment building is legal not physical. Your attorney will draw up and file the condominium declaration and by-laws which establish your building as a condominium.

Since each unit of a condominium is individually owned, each unit must have its own survey. In addition, the common areas, such as the hallways and foyer, must be surveyed. Surveys of this type are frequently plottings of air space.

The by-laws are the rules and regulations by which the condominium homeowner's association govern its activities. They establish owner's rights, duties, voting and administration policy. In general, a large condominium development will have an elected board of condo owners which then hires an outside management firm to run the day-to-day operations of the condominium. The management firm is then accountable to the condo owner's association. With a smaller condominium, the elected board will supervise operations without the services of an outside management firm.

The cost of renovation depends upon the original condition of the building; however, an economy can be achieved by remodeling by tier. Many converters recommend that a great deal of attention be paid to the kitchen and baths. This makes good sense since it is these rooms that sell any home. These are also the rooms that become most easily dated. A large, modern kitchen with the best appliances and a bath with modern fixtures is a major expense for the converter. However, this investment is returned in quicker sales and a higher profit.

You can adjust the price of your units according to market conditions, and with a successful conversion, with brisk sales, the last few units may sell for a higher price. This can be viewed as a bonus to the successful converter.

THE CHICAGO EXPERIENCE

The Chicago area is the most active area for residential condominium conversion. An expertise has been developed by condo converters in Chicago that is unique in this country. In 1973 there were about 19,000 residential condominiums in the Chicago area. By 1978 there were approximately 66,000 and much of this increase was due to conversions. In spite of a maturing market, the demand for condos close to the city's center is still strong.

Chicago's mature market has a few interesting characteristics. They are worth remembering, since in years to come, the same conditions will be true in other urban areas.

• Prices are high and in some cases $100 per square foot. This is higher than the cost to reproduce. I suspect the desire of the typical Chicago condo buyer for an older, smaller building with an unduplicable "charm" is responsible for this market curiosity.

• The cost of an apartment building suitable for conversion has increased from 4 to 6 times gross annual income to 7 to 10 times gross annual income. This makes the apartment seller a de facto partner of the converter with the additional advantage of taking his profits in the form of capital gains.

• Converters, acting in their own economic interests, have, as a bonus effect, reversed the trend toward blight in many sections of the city. This has made Chicago one of the few major cities that can boast of a returning middle class.

• The condominium conversion has now become a political issue.

The success of condo conversion in Chicago has as much to do with the initiative of local converters as the enlightenment of city administrators. Chicago has a model condominium ordinance which requires the converter to effect real not cosmetic building improvements and protects the rights of tenants and buyers.

It is a fact of life that the quality of a neighborhood depends on the degree of owner occupants. Landlords, and to a lesser degree, tenants, have only a passing interest in local civic affairs. The absentee or temporary nature of their involvement makes it diffi-

cult for them to develop a real interest in such issues as schools
and city services.

The condo converter can take pride in making center-city home
ownership a possibility to a wide market and, in so doing, improving entire neighborhoods. The city can take equal pride in restoring these neighborhoods to their highest and best use* and, in
so doing, increase its tax collections. Each condo unit is taxed
individually and the total taxes collected on the entire building far
exceed its taxes as an apartment building.

Condo conversion is not only an excellent investment but satisfies even the most souped-up social conscience. The converter,
tradesman, attorney and banker, motivated by free market forces,
can and has accomplished what government has so far found
elusive.

The alternative is to let a situation continue in our cities in
which buildings are managed by many uncaring landlords, or
worse, slumlords.

Now, for the bad news. In Chicago, condo conversion has
relived, at 78 r.p.m., the history of many older industries. The
railroad industry is an example in technicolor. The pattern is
as follows: a tentative and experimental stage followed by a
period of growth coupled with abuses by a few fast-buck cre-
tins, followed by corrective legislation, followed by boom years,
followed by politically motivated persecution. This pattern
finally ends with inefficient and humiliating government controls.

Chicago is currently in the political persecution stage of development. The whip is being cracked by the populist politicians.
Once again, they are mustering out the image of the poor and
disabled to troop the colors on their behalf. Neither the poor nor
disabled are directly involved since a building with low rents is
not suitable conversion property, but in an area where a conver-

---

*That use of land which will yield the greatest return and, thereby, develop the
highest land value.

sion takes place a better enviroment soon develops.

The political future of residential condominiums in Chicago has yet to be resolved. However, I believe the trend to condominiums is, in every major metropolitan area, unstoppable.

CHAPTER 11

*S*UBDIVIDING

Under all is the land.
Upon its wise utilization and
widely allocated ownership
depend the survival and
growth of free institutions
and of our civilization.

—Preamble, Realtor Code of Ethics

$L$and has a value only if it can be used and it is the role of the subdivider and land developer to enhance that use, and therefore the value of land. The supply of land is fixed by Mother Nature but population is determined by man (a more whimsical entity). This increased demand for land not only increases its value but creates pressure to change land's use—agriculture lands change to residential.

This chapter concerns itself with the steps necessary to change land use. The buying of raw or undeveloped land and dividing it into smaller, buildable lots is the job of the subdivider.

Subdividing is, and will continue to become, a complex procedure requiring many skills and an active full-time participation. For this reason, it is not a passive investment but a business venture. The profit potential is enormous and so is the risk.

The problem lies in dealing with state and local government bodies. Their concern for health, safety, environment and orderly growth are, of course, legitimate. One only has to look at areas built in an age when subdivisions were scratched out on a dinner napkin to get the point. However, the maze of regulations together with the narrow, no-growth and unimaginative attitude of some local authorities make subdividing a challenge to one's powers of patience and persuasiveness. In addition, time (money) spent for various approvals is, at the least, frustrating. The philosophy of intelligent town planning is often mocked in implementation.

The rapid expansion of urban areas, the universal concern for the environment, the demand for more and better public facilities and services, coupled with the pressure of taxes, have added to the complexities of subdividing.

And yet, it is these complexities and the player's understanding of the local market, and most of all local, personalities and moods, that present opportunities for the small investor.

Large, national builders, due to the scale of their operation, are interested in developing large tracts of land for residential, commercial or industrial use. The small, say 5- to 25-acre, residential development is a waste of their considerable talent and resources. It's like asking Einstein to play tic-tac-toe. The subdividing of small residential developments has historically been done by the small, local or regional builder as a collateral activity to his primary job of building. However, the small- and medium-sized builder is no longer interested in the aggravation, delay and red tape involved in what has become a new and distinct profession of subdividing. The typical builder likes to build and avoid as much as possible the "briefcase arts." To put it another way, local builders like to buy property in an approved, subdivided and ready-to-build condition and they will pay for the privilege.

SITE SELECTION

The first step is to select a parcel suitable for development. Keeping in contact with a number of real estate brokers may be of help to you with site selection, and many desirable properties can be found by just "cruising." These small tracts of vacant land can still be found in and around expanding urban areas although it's quite possible that the land is undeveloped for a reason. Easy land, like easy oil, is developed first. The difficulties could have been one of soil condition, location, land contour, absence of nearby utility services, or access. This doesn't mean difficult land should be forgotten, as a changing market, higher prices, and improved technology may now make problem land economically feasible.

The investor should not be too concerned about the property being advertised for sale. The owners of most vacant property are sellers if the sale price makes sense to them. The problem, of course, is, does their sale price make sense to you.

DETERMINING A PURCHASE PRICE FOR RAW LAND

Assuming you have found property you consider suitable for development, it's a good idea to first get the best estimate of the value of the property in an approved, ready-to-build state. Your real estate broker is the best source of this appraisal and his services are free. Make sure his appraisal considers future value, say one year, in his calculations as it may take this long for approvals and ultimate sale. Once you know this figure, divide it in half in order to arrive at a purchase figure. You can go higher if conditions are ideal and your original purchase offer should be less because—well—it just may be accepted. Nevertheless, this figure is one in which you can reasonably expect to cover all costs (including the unanticipated) plus provide a respectable profit for your time, knowledge and enterprise.

Before actually making the offer, three other areas must be investigated.

1. *Financing feasibility.* For reasons which I will shortly explain, a preliminary and verbal commitment on financing from a lender is necessary before entering into a contract. This is unlike buying a home, in which a sales contract is signed first with your ability to get a mortgage as a contingency.

2. *Municipal agency rules, regulations and ordinances.* Manuals are available at a nominal charge from your local city hall or county building regarding policies and procedures for obtaining building permits, construction approvals for roads and utilities, inspections, environmental regulations, and other requirements. In addition, most local jurisdictions have an information officer who can readily answer any of your questions. At this time it is also a good idea to make an estimate of the fees involved. In some areas they are quite high and, while this will seldom be a reason to abandon the venture, it does help your arithmetic.

3. *Time.* Time is money and time spent waiting for various approvals should also be estimated. A knowledge of time involved in previous developments within the same jurisdiction is a good guide for the subdivider.

If, through your investigation, a financial or regulatory problem seems insurmountable, you may have to abandon the venture. If, however, the idea seems feasible, then make your offer.

THE OFFER

The most advantageous offer you can make is an option, or better yet, a series of renewable options. The option money should be as little as possible and, if the sale ultimately goes through, should be applied to the purchase price. The option is only a right to purchase property at an agreed-upon price and terms within a specific time. This eliminates much of the risk entailed in development. If for some reason the venture runs into a snag, the optionee loses nothing more than his option money. There's no way he can get stuck with undevelopable property.

Another alternative is to enter into a joint venture agreement with the seller. The advantage to this is the complete elimination of risk by having little or none of your money invested. The disadvantage is that you have acquired a business partner who shares in the profits and who may or may not be compatible with you.

With either the option or joint venture agreement, the services of a real estate attorney are essential.

SITE PLANNING

Once you've optioned the property for three months to a year, it's time for site planning. For this, you will need the services of a site planner and/or civil engineer. It's a good idea to select a local engineering firm familiar with local conditions. The importance of dealing locally cannot be overemphasized. The engineering problems encountered are rarely complicated in a technical sense but get quite involved when dealing with the labyrinth of public and private procedures and personalities. A local firm is better able to deal with these subtleties.

The engineers report will include:

1. A description of the size and boundaries of the property obtained from local land records. This description should include the location of the property in relation to access roads, shopping, schools, churches, present or future transit systems and parks.

2. A field investigation including a description of the topography (land contour), flood plains, drainage problems, erosion problems, obvious soil conditions and various other physical features such as trees, streams, views or rock formation.

3. A description of the present zoning and, more important, an opinion of the feasibility of a zoning change. Nearly all development property requires a zoning change, at least to accommodate a higher density. Even though the sales contract is written contingent upon this zoning change, many months or years (money) can be wasted waiting for an approval which may not come. An informal discussion over lunch with a key member of the zoning or planning commission (in many cases they are the same) can give you a sense of the possible. Unless a rezoning to your use has a reasonable chance of success, abandon the idea. The engineer's discussion of present and proposed zoning definitions should include minimum lot size, frontage, setbacks, population densities, height limitations and other pertinent facts.

4. Availability of utilities. Sewer, water, gas, electricity and telephone should be discussed in depth. It is important to know not only if they are available but under what circumstances and at what cost to the developer. Like all aspects of development, policies vary widely throughout the country.

5. Roads affecting the site. Roads fronting the property or roads planned to give access to the property should be discussed together with an estimate of improvement costs, if any.

6. Streets within the development. Local construction standards of streets within the development should be discussed together with a preliminary cost estimate.

7. Schools. The availability or, more precisely, the unavailability of schools should be discussed. Lack of school facilities often precludes zoning. It is now a custom for the developer to be responsible in some way for providing adequate schools. He may be required to donate land for a school site, as well as a cash contribution.

8. Topographic map. The topographic map is one of the more important entries in the engineer's report. It gives the contour of

the land at predetermined (1-foot to 10-foot) intervals and is essential in understanding the degree of natural drainage and in determining the amount and cost of site grading (earthwork movement).

9. Soil Test. Soil conditions are of importance for the determination of design for road beds, utility lines, foundation supports and for dealing with soil erosion problems.

With the engineer's report in hand, you can now do the arithmetic. Remember you are still in the option period and have made no final agreement to purchase. And don't forget the estimate of time to bring the project to conclusion as part of your arithmetic.

If the project makes mathematical sense then it's time for a surveyor to draw up a preliminary subdivision plat. In so doing, the surveyor will take into consideration the findings of the engineering report. He will use the minimum lot size of the proposed zoning change to work out the optimum number of lots. However, for your preliminary work, you can estimate that 20 percent of the raw land, when subdivided, will be devoted to streets. When the remaining 80 percent is divided by the minimum lot size, you will have the approximate number of lots, less allowances for park, schools, municipal facilities (wells, etc.) and areas for drainage and bad soil.

PUBLIC HEARINGS

You are now ready for a public hearing. This entails a presentation of your development plans before the zoning board or planning commission. Your market study, engineering report, and survey together with your previous informal meeting with key board members should make you well prepared to give an intelligent, positive, persuasive and winning argument. Nevertheless, problems always develop. The problems can come from the public or various board members.

Much of this public and official hysteria can be calmed by an intelligent, well-organized, detailed, and open discussion of the merits of your plan. However, you must remember that any project, no matter how well planned and beneficial to the area, will not stop anyone intent on mischievous public yodeling.

The precise nature of their objections vary with local circumstances but the following are common:

1. Many communities try to maintain a rural, low-density environment even though the area is in the path of growth. Their true interest is exclusion no matter what their other arguments.

2. In many areas, planning commissions and zoning boards are interested in promoting industrial, commercial and multifamily development. Since these properties are viewed as more taxable, a single family development may not be in the stars.

3. Outdated zoning and subdivision regulations, rigidly applied, create a stifling of innovation by the developer.

4. A "What's in it for me?" attitude in many communities frequently translates to demands for unneeded park donations, etc., from the developer.

5. Concern for a subdivision's impact on local schools and taxes is always a legitimate concern.

6. Many communities want to know *who* is going to live in the subdivision rather than what it will look like.

7. A concern for the subdivision's effect on surrounding property values is also legitimate.

As a result of these hearings and their attendant adjustments and compromises along the way, a final plan can be drawn up and approved. The approved subdivision plat is then recorded. You now have an option (or you may previously have exercised your option and purchased) on land approved for a residential subdivision.

The change brought about by subdividing has been legal, not physical, and as such, the property has a value considerably in excess of the purchase price. This excess is the subdivider's profit.

I've used the example of the single-family subdivision but the same principles would apply for commercial, industrial and multifamily development.

The following is an example of the numbers involved in subdividing:

If we assume a 10-acre parcel of raw land
can be bought (optioned) for $12,000 per acre

THEN

10 acres at $12,000 per acre	$120,000
Option money (6 months)	$5,000
Approximate number of lots	20
Average sale price per lot in an approved condition	$12,000

Costs (Estimated)

Engineering	$12,000
Surveying	2,000
Legal	1,000
Soil Tests	2,000
Filing Costs	2,000
Accounting and Misc.	1,000
Total Cost to bring to approval	$20,000 Total Costs
Raw Land Costs	$120,000
Costs to bring to approved state	20,000
Total Investment	$140,000
Sale price per lot $12,000 × 20	$240,000
	−140,000
Profit to subdivider	$100,000

Should the subdivider wish to become a land developer and thus
make the physical improvements necessary (streets, sewers, sidewalks, utilities, etc.) and if we assume $10,000 per lot in improve-
ment costs, then:

Land and costs to bring to approval	$140,000
Improvements Costs $10,000 × 20	200,000
	$340,000

TOTAL INVESTMENT IN READY TO BUILD LAND

Estimated sale price of improved lot $23,000 × 20

Total Sale Price	= $460,000
Total Investment	−340,000
Profit to land developer	$120,000

Your natural sales market for this type of property is the local
builder. You can begin looking for builder-buyers at any time
during the chain of events leading to approval that you can establish a price. In many cases, the builder, being aware of your

intentions, will contact you. He, unlike the general public, understands that on the eighth day God did not subdivide.

You can of course continue to develop the property by contracting for streets, sewers, etc. but for this you'll need a construction loan. To continue to develop land including the construction and sale of homes will further increase your return but also dramatically extend your risk.

SUMMARY

A small parcel of land is of no interest to the large developer and the small builder doesn't want to be bothered. It is this fact that presents opportunities for the subdivider.

The entire venture should be so structured as to have as little money invested as possible. This is done by the use of the option or partnership agreement with the seller.

The deal should also be structured in a logical order with incremental risks. In this way a serious problem requiring abandonment of the venture will minimize loss.

The services of a civil engineer and surveyor are absolutely essential and it is equally essential that they be local. This ensures that they will be familiar with local regulations, personalities, procedures, and politics.

Subdividing is easy, hard or impossible depending on the jurisdiction. No discussion of subdividing and land development can cover the infinite local variables. Local politics or more accurately, local socio-politico-eco instincts, has become extremely important and its effects on development can be understood only on a local level. To a large extent, development is as much an exercise in persuasion as it is engineering. The ideal land-development team would be a combination of Frank Lloyd Wright, Niccolò Machiavelli, Sigmund Freud and P. T. Barnum, with the latter working overtime.

I think that it is also important to mention that land regulation, although, still local in nature, is tending to become a state, regional, or even national concern. I believe the future will bring a more uniform body of land use regulation.

CHAPTER 12

*I*NCOME PROPERTY

Capitalism's most pleasant offshoot is political freedom.
—Author

*T*his chapter covers a few of the many types of small and intermediate investments. A sensible decision for you may depend on your interests, market, investment capital or a special opportunity that presents itself. No type of investment is, by nature, good or bad. An investment is only good or bad in relation to you. For example, I prefer a neighborhood shopping center as a good intermediate investment. However, your circumstances may show that an investment in vacation property, with all its seasonal problems, may be better.

VACANT LAND

Investing in vacant land may or may not be attractive to the average investor. Although land in general will continue to appreciate due to increasing demand and fixed supply, there are a number of risks the investor should consider before investing.

Among these risks is the difficulty of obtaining favorable (high-leverage) financing. Lending institutions do not like to make loans on land held for long-term investment due to the nonincome-producing nature of vacant land. When they do make these types of loans, the down payment is at least 50 percent with a five- to 12-year term and at a higher rate than income-producing property. Not only does the mortgaged investor have a monthly debt service (principal and interest) payment, but taxes, liability insurance and the possibility of a special assessment add to his monthly cash outflow.

Secondly, since land cannot be depreciated, the tax-shelter benefits of real estate are severely curtailed.

And finally, since favorable financing and much of the tax-shelter and income benefits are missing, only appreciation (due to inflation or higher use) is left as an investment motive. The land will, in all probability, be worth more in the future, but will it be enough to compensate the investor for his cash drain in the interim? If the parcel is situated in the path of city growth, how long will it take for it to be worth developing? It's a high-risk investment.

If we take the example of five acres of land bought for $30,000 and held for ten years and if we assume a $15,000 mortgage at 11 percent for ten years with liability insurance of $20 per year and taxes at $400 per year, then:

HOLDING COSTS

Debt service $206.70 per month	
$206.70 × 12 × 10	$24,804
Taxes $400 × 10	4,000
Liability insurance $20 × 10	200
Holding costs	$29,004

Assuming the parcel is sold for triple its original sale price ($90,000) ten years later, your return on your $15,000 original investment (before taxes and excluding closing costs) is less than 8 percent compounded.

Depending on the parcel, certain actions can be taken by the investor to derive some interim income. In most cases, it won't be enough to cover the holding costs but it helps. Here are some ideas:

RURAL ACREAGE

1. Sale of timber, gravel, sand, peat, topsoil
2. Rental income from a tenant farmer (this type of parcel must be large)
3. Christmas trees (this takes 4 to 6 years to be economic)
4. Rental income from a mobile-home complex

URBAN AND SUBURBAN LAND

1. Parking lot
2. Miniature golf
3. Driving range

If a parcel of land is widely known to be developed within four to five years, the chances are the market has already adjusted for this, or to put it another way, if you know the property has great potential, the seller does too. Great buys are not that common. Of course, the investor can significantly increase the value of his investment if, during the holding period, he can have the property rezoned to a higher (more intense) use (i.e., agricultural land rezoned to residential or residential to commercial or commercial to industrial).

Buying land for long-term investment rather than immediate need can make good sense if the investor has some inside or special knowledge. For example, the investor may know of a major employer's plans to move into the area. This would stimulate residential and commercial demand for nearby land.

Another advantage to land investment is the passive nature of the enterprise. No management, maintenance or repair is involved. All you have to do is write out the checks and settle for a modest return.

SINGLE-FAMILY HOME INVESTMENT

I once knew an "investor" who had accumulated considerable equity, at least $150,000, by the simple expedient of never having sold his previous residences. He wasn't what could be called an active real estate investor, he just considered selling any home he lived in "too much of a bother." His six moves were initiated by either a job transfer or a desire to upgrade and in each case he had just enough money for the minimum down payment on his next home. All of his previous homes were successfully rented with the tenants responsible for all utilities and most maintenance costs. The accidental nature of his "investment strategy" makes me wonder what he could have done if he had tried.

For obvious reasons, single-family homes are highly rentable. The problem with this type of investment, like apartments, is that the rent in the early years of ownership is frequently lower than your monthly payment. This negative cash flow can get quite disturbing if it is too high, say $100 per month.

For this reason, it makes good sense to buy homes in need of rehabilitation. If you keep in close contact with your local broker, he may notify you when this type of property becomes available. The FHA and VA publish lists of foreclosures in your area. Nearly all of these foreclosures are run-down and are bought on an "as is," sealed-bid, basis. Banks and savings and loan associations are another good source of foreclosured property. These properties are invariably good buys as these institutions are not in the real estate or rehabilitation business; their only interest is to get rid of these vacant properties and at any price that will at least return their mortgage investment.

Maintenance costs are also higher with a single-family home as opposed to an apartment unit. However, a rent reduction can be used to accommodate lawn care and/or painting.

TOWN HOUSE AND CONDOMINIUM RENTALS

Buying and renting a condominium or town house may be more appealing to an investor than a single-family residence or apartment building. The reasons for this are:

1. Exterior and common-ground maintenance is handled by management (for a fee).

2. Most condo and town-house developments offer amenities that are uneconomic in the small apartment complex. This makes them more rentable.

3. Three- and four-bedroom town houses are commonly available. This rental market cannot be served by apartments. Many town houses also have basements, thereby solving an inherent problem with apartment and condo living—storage.

4. It is customary for management of resort condos to not only maintain the property but to rent the units on a weekly or monthly basis when the owner is not in residence. This makes good sense to anyone who enjoys seeing others pay for (at least in part) his vacation home.

Care should be taken to read the condominium by-laws in order to determine if the units are allowed to be rented and under what circumstances.

APARTMENT BUILDINGS

In spite of the advantage of ownership, renting continues to be the preferred form of shelter to an increasing number of people. Young married couples, swingles and the elderly continue to account for much of the demand.

Apartment buildings fall into three general classifications: high-rise elevator buildings of four stories or more, low-rise walk-ups of three stories or less, and garden-type, low-rise buildings on sizable parcels of land. Your local market factors determine the type, size and style of the building. Among these factors are land costs, zoning regulations and local demand.

The small- and medium-size investor's interests range from the two-flat or duplex to, say, a fifty-unit building. It is this range that I will discuss.

FINANCING

Conventional financing is commonly available with a 25 percent down payment and a 25-year term. A land contract sale, wrap-around mortgage or purchase with a land lease are also common methods of financing apartment buildings. Another interesting method of financing this type of investment not previously discussed is a combination of a first mortgage from a lending institution (insurance company) and a second mortgage held by the seller. This type of financing dramatically increases your leverage and, of course, reduces your cash flow (income). If we assume a 10-unit apartment building sells for $250,000, the normal down payment required would be 25 percent of the purchase price or $62,500. However, if the seller is willing to hold a second (junior) mortgage for, say, $40,000, then your investment would only be $22,500 plus closing costs.

COSTS AND INCOME

Operating costs on an apartment building are all costs of operation except principal and interest payment on the mortgage loan. These operating costs may include gas, electric, water, insurance, garbage disposal, repair, maintenance, payroll and taxes. In most cases, taxes are the largest single cost and total operating expenses may account for as much as 50 percent of the gross income.

As was mentioned earlier, in many major markets, with a 25 percent down payment on a small- or medium-size apartment building, and in the early years of ownership, expecting a cash flow is pure fantasy. A good goal for the investor is to try to break even, but even this is becoming elusive. In time (two to five years), the investor, assuming periodic rent increases and relatively constant operating costs, will begin to show a profit. In spite of this, apartment buildings are still a solid investment. The tax-shelter benefits, the potential for future conversion to condominium, appreciation and equity payoff more than compensate the investor for a small or even slightly negative cash flow.

APARTMENT TIPS

Many investors supplement their incomes with vending machines, coin-operated laundries and garage rentals. Vending machines do best in a building with younger tenants, and coin laundries are a valuable service in any building. It's best to contract these concessions out as 1) it eliminates maintenance headaches and 2) it doesn't give the tenant the impression that you're trying to vacuum in every last dime from his estate. (You are.)

As a buyer, it is essential that you verify every figure told to you by the seller or his agent. Listen to everything and believe nothing. This may include the vacancy rate, gross income, taxes, operating expenses or the status of the heater, roof, etc.

The addition of a swimming pool, sauna or tennis court may or may not make sense to the investor. If these amenities guarantee full occupancy in a competitive market with a high vacancy rate, if the added expenses can be quickly retrieved by higher rents or if the market characteristics are such that these features are expected, then they should be added.

Let's take an example of a swimming pool costing $12,000, with a 10-year useful life and let's assume a maintenance cost of $75 per month including repairs and chemicals. The cost per unit per month on a 40-unit building would then be:

Original cost	$12,000
Divided by useful life of 10 years	1,200 per year
Maintenance per year ($75 × 12)	900 per year
Annual pool cost	$2,100
Cost per unit, per month	
$2,100 ÷ 12 ÷ 40	$4.38

If the addition of the pool will add $5.00 per unit per month in added rent, then the pool addition justifies the expenses. If the pool would cut down the vacancy level by one unit per month, it is also worth the expense (assuming an average rent of $275). Likewise, the pool is probably a bad investment to a 10-unit building as this would require a rent increase of $17.50 per unit per month and your market may not accept this.

Low-cost amenities such as picnic tables, patio furniture or flower beds for tenant use are always worth their nominal cost.

Before buying any apartment building consider its convertibility into condominiums. It's safe to say that any newer, well-constructed and -designed apartment building has a future potential for conversion. The current market conditions may not be right but someday they will. You may not wish to convert it but whoever buys the building from you may. If it has this potential, you will invariably realize a higher resale price.

MINI-WAREHOUSES

A mini-warehouse is a motel for things. The concept is only about 20 years old and in the last five years has shown tremendous growth. Today, many major population areas have minis and I believe this investment has an excellent growth potential.

The reasons for the increasing demand for small, short-term storage are growing. The list of users could never be complete but the following are some of the demand factors:

1. The condominium, mobile home and apartment generally have inadequate storage space. In addition, builders of medium-

priced housing, in order to hold down prices, have eliminated storage areas (basements and sometimes attics) in their design.

2. The increasing popularity of the trappings of leisure such as trailers, boats and snow mobiles.

3. The demand by small retailers for more space for inventory.

4. The increasing demands of recordkeeping (sooner or later this means outside storage) by many businesses and professions (i.e., banks, local government, lawyers, doctors, retailers).

5. The increasingly higher crime rate demands secure storage for valuables such as antiques, particularly during an absence by the owner.

6. An increasingly mobile society which requires temporary furniture storage between moves.

CONSTRUCTION

The exterior of a mini-warehouse gives the impression of a string of garages housed under one flat roof. This is not far from the truth. Construction of this type of building is either of concrete block or steel with the same materials used for interior walls. The entire building sits on a four-inch reinforced concrete slab. This concrete base also has a slight slope for drainage. Ceilings are generally 10 feet high with a metal roof. A .5- to .75-inch spray insulation is applied inside the structure for moisture resistance. Seven- to ten-foot overhead steel doors are used for the larger units and a three-foot-wide steel door for the smaller units. The only utility service provided is electricity to support one light bulb on a pull chain. In a few northern areas with severe winters, heat is also supplied on an extra-charge basis. Driveways are paved and the entire outside area is best lit with mercury-vapor lamps. A six- to eight-foot chain-link fence with one gate and sometimes barbed wire strung along the top surrounds the entire complex.

LOCATION

At least a two-acre site on a major thoroughfare is ideal. A large traffic count (available from your local highway department) gives your project and advertising billboard a high visibility. A location not more than fifteen minutes driving time from a high concentration of apartment buildings, mobile-home parks or condominiums is crucial. And, finally, investigate the degree, if any, of competition and be sure also to investigate local rental rates and vacancy rates.

Two acres of land will accommodate one acre under roof (rentable space). The remainder is used for driveways, fence, rental office and possibly a resident manager's apartment.

SECURITY

Each tenant buys his own padlock and is solely responsible for locking his unit. In addition to the fence and barbed wire, it's a good idea to let a few naughty doggies roam the premises during closing hours. Their purpose being to a) warn or b) chew on any potential mischief-maker.

INSURANCE

Just as with any other type of real estate, the mini-warehouse must have adequate fire and liability coverage. If a manager is involved, he must be insured for workmen's compensation. However, since tenants are solely responsible for handling their items, they, not you, are advised to have adequate insurance coverage for their contents. Most minis, in addition to making a small profit on the sale of padlocks, sell tenants this type of insurance. The rates vary from $1.00 to $2.00 per month per $1,000 of valuation.

MANAGEMENT

In most cases, the manager lives on the premises as this provides for more attentive management. The manager's apartment should be at least a two-bedroom, 1,000-square-foot unit with all the amenities common to apartments in the area. This apartment is generally rent-free and is considered a part of his wages. All the duties and responsibilities of the manager are the same as for other property management.

FINANCING

Since minis are a relatively new investment, many lenders are hesitant to take a chance on financing, and when they do, they generally charge the maximum interest rate. The securing of this type of loan may require some shopping and salesmanship by the investor.

UNIT SIZE

The mini-warehouse should have units in varying sizes. It's a good idea to have some units of closet size while a few should contain 1,000 square feet with most being in the 150-square-foot range. Your own local market knowledge will decide the mix.

OPERATION

Most mini-warehouse complexes require one month's rent in advance and a security deposit also equal to one month's rent. This should give enough protection against delinquent rent. In the event of nonpayment of rent, most states allow for a warehouse-man's lien on the personal property of the tenant. This may ultimately result in a public auction to satisfy the debt.

Other income which may be derived from this type of operation include, in addition to padlock and insurance sales, pallet rental, truck rental, vending machines, outdoor storage space and pay telephones.

A principal attraction of the mini-warehouse investment is the minimum maintenance involved. Most of these costs are devoted to maintaining the manager's apartment and rental office.

Advertising is also low considering the size of the operation. An ad in the Yellow Pages and a billboard on the premises are the most effective forms of advertisement.

THE ARITHMETIC

There are too many variables involved to accurately figure the return on investment in minis. Land costs, construction costs, rental rates, real estate taxes and management fees vary widely across the country. Nevertheless construction costs per square foot are lower for this type of building than any other type of construction. The following is only an example of costs and return.

INVESTMENT

Land cost	$ 50,000
Improvement costs: 45,000-sq.-ft. bldg., paving, sewer, lights, fence, architect at $13 per sq. ft.	$562,500
Closing costs	15,000
Total cost	$627,500
Minus 75% mortgage	− 470,625
Equal total investment required	$156,875

ANNUAL RETURN

Gross income: 45,000 sq. ft. @ $.28 per sq. ft. per month	$151,200
Minus 15% for vacancy and bad debts	$22,680
Equal gross operating income	$128,520
Expenses including taxes, insurance, management fee, maintenance, utilities and advertising (expenses on minis average 30% of gross operating income)	$ 38,520
Equal return before debt service	$ 90,000
Minus principal and interest on mortgage balance at 10½%, 20 years	− $ 56,344
Equal annual cash flow	$ 33,656

Return on investment 21.5%

Mini-warehousing is a relatively new concept and new ideas and procedures are being introduced every year. In order to keep current on this rapidly changing field, a trade association called the Self-Service Storage Association of Dayton, Ohio, has been formed.

SMALL SHOPPING CENTERS

In the last 25 years, the shopping center has replaced the neighborhood store as the principal American marketplace. Its growth potential is limited only by the limits of residential development.

There are three types of shopping centers and they can be distinguished by size or by the type of key tenant.

TYPE OF CENTER	KEY TENANT
Neighborhood	Supermarket or convenience market
Community	Junior department store or variety store
Regional	Full-line department store

The average investor is interested only in the neighborhood center. This type of center typically has a site size of one to five acres with rentable space ranging from 7,000 to 30,000 square feet. The stores are one-story, contiguous and in a straight row, U-shaped or L-shaped. The parking lot and rear delivery area account for about 60 percent of the total site. For this type of center to be economically feasible, it must draw from an area having about 1,000 families.

Almost any small business would be attracted to this type of center. The following are some of the common tenants:

Convenience food market	Ice-cream store
Supermarket	Speciality store
Bakery	Florist
Restaurant	Gift shop
Liquor store	Drugstore
Take-out food	Coin laundry
Barber shop	Real estate office
Dry cleaners	Beauty shop
Children's wear	Shoe store

If you consider condominium conversion a business venture rather than an investment then I think the neighborhood shopping center is currently the best investment of all. Someday, I suppose, the neighborhood center will be overbuilt, but this doesn't seem likely in the foreseeable future. I think a comparison between the neighborhood shopping center and the apartment building investment is useful in explaining this point.

The per-square-foot construction costs of a small shopping center are considerably less than apartment-building construction. The typical building is of a brick-veneered cement-block exterior, dry-wall-covered cement-block interior partitions, no basement and flat roof. The tenant generally endures the costs of carpeting or floor tile, the air conditioner and in-store partitions. In addition, the tenants buy all trade fixtures such as counters, shelving, freezers and window treatments.

Using my own market as an example, the apartment building can be constructed for about $38 per square foot while shopping-center construction runs about $26 per square foot. Neither figure includes land costs. Although due to a higher zoning, land costs for a shopping center are somewhat higher, it is never enough to make up the 50 percent increase in construction costs.

And yet, despite the difference in construction costs, retail space rents for more per square foot. To put it another way, a shopping center can be built for one third less and rented for one third more per square foot than an apartment building.

Operating expenses account for a lesser portion of gross rents in a shopping center. The owner is generally responsible for property taxes and building insurance. The tenants are typically responsible for all utilities, including outdoor lighting, garbage disposal and parking-lot maintenance but not repair. The tenants usually share this maintenance expense on a pro-rata basis. With the typical apartment building, 50 percent of the gross rent pays the operating expenses while with the shopping center about 30 percent is usual.

Shopping centers also require the minimum of management and supervisory duties. A neighborhood center can easily be managed by the owner. These duties include securing tenants, arranging for major repair work and rent collection. In all other ways, the building runs itself.

A shopping center also has a lower tenant turnover than the apartment. It is customary for a retailer to sign a three- to five-year lease with ten years not being uncommon. This type of long-term lease carries an escalation clause which requires the tenant to pay for any increase in taxes or insurance during the term of the lease. In addition, most retail leases give the owner an additional inflation hedge by being percentage leases. This type of lease requires a minimum fixed rental fee plus a percentage of the tenant's gross or net income in excess of a stated minimum. For example, if the lease terms are $1,000 per month plus 5 percent of gross sales in excess of $25,000, then a month in which the tenant grosses $30,-000 would require him to pay $1,250 rent.

More than half of the rental income in these centers comes from large national or local chain stores with top credit ratings.

Unless an area is excessively competitive, the vacancy rate of these centers is less than the apartment rate in the surrounding area. I suspect the reason for this is the popular urge to own a business and be one's own boss. There will always be a demand from small businessmen for small retail space.

Due to relatively low construction costs, high rentals, low vacancy rate and low maintenance costs, this type of investment, unlike the apartment building, should show a cash flow in the early years of ownership. This income, due to the escalation clause, is protected from inflation and with the percentage leases will increase over the years.

I highly recommend this type of investment.

SUMMARY

Like any grocer's son, I wake every morning ready to teach. And yet for you, I teach from ignorance. I know nothing about you, your income, talents, cash reserves, goals and, most of all, I know nothing about your market. This is your business. Nevertheless, I can't resist offering an investment plan which will suit the most humble. Man's (my) most uncontrollable, infuriating and harmless instinct is meddling.

Your first investment should always be your own home. Custom demands that young people first rent an apartment, but mathematics indicate otherwise. A low down-payment loan is advisable at this stage. A VA loan is the best as it requires no down payment, but if you're not eligible then one of the FHA loans will do. A medium-price-range home can be bought for a down payment of $1,000 to $4,000 and creative financing can be applied.

Although a low down payment means a high monthly mortgage payment, I wouldn't let this disturb you. You can treat all mortgage payments not as a monthly expense but rather as a forced savings program with a home thrown in as a bonus. The increase in your equity over the years may equal or exceed your total monthly payments. In a certain sense, those who have bought homes in the last ten years have lived for free.

In areas with a high cost of housing, a town house or a condominium may be the best choice as a first home or, if you are up to it, a home in need of rehabilitation. In any event, within three to five years you'll be ready for another real estate transaction. You can move to a larger home—by this time your family situation may compel it—or you can buy income property. One thing is certain: You will by this time have enough equity in your home to do either. The rental property you buy may be as small as a town house or condo and may extend up to, say, a ten-unit apartment building. If you buy a larger home, think location. If you buy an apartment building, think conversion. Your down payment can come from savings, refinancing your existing home or you can sell your original home and become a live-in owner in an apartment building. And in any real estate transaction—big or small—never forget the seller's ability to help in your financing. This may come in the form of a land contract sale, a second mortgage held by the seller or a decorating allowance.

Intermediate investments may be done alone or in partnership with others. They include large apartment buildings, condo conversions, land development, shopping centers, mini-warehouses, mobile-home parks, medical centers or small office buildings. Other investments are available to the imaginative investor who thoroughly understands his market. For example, I have seen old warehouses converted into small indoor shopping centers where a shop is called a shoppe and a 300-foot-high mound of garbage converted into a profit-making ski slope.

Don't be afraid to be creative in your investment approach. Many outstanding investments have been made by investors who have picked up ideas in travels to other parts of the country or the world. These ideas have been brought home and adapted to local market conditions.

An interesting avenue to explore is the condominiumization of a small shopping center. There seems to be a strong and untapped market for the retail condo, it's legally possible, and yet I know of no case in which it has been done.

Expansion is more important in the early years of investment than income. In time, income will be generated due to periodic rent increases.

The type of investment course you take depends on you and your local market factors, but if you continually seek expansion, you will find that your net worth will soon begin to grow geometrically.

CHAPTER 13

ET CETERA

Et cetera, et cetera, et cetera . . .
—The King and I

H. L. Mencken defined wealth as making $100 a year more than your brother-in-law. I can't quarrel with this but I think it's much more. It means you don't have to eat meat without a bone attached, have a B.Y.O. party, spell your name to the maître d', pick up another dinner check or wait in line for anything. In short, you don't have to live at wholesale.

I believe the surest, quickest, easiest road to wealth for the average man is real estate investment. Nevertheless, anything that sounds too good to be true—is. I have, therefore, saved the negative factors of real estate for this last chapter in the hope you wouldn't notice. To balance this, I also present a sure-fire way to avoid these problems.

I will indulge in some prophecy regarding real estate based on current trends, and finally, as an afterthought, I will divulge the secret for bringing complete order, peace, justice and tranquility to every land under the heavenly dome.

SELLING A VACANT HOME

The best of homes, when vacant, like people without suntans, show all the blemishes (i.e., behind every picture there is a nail hole). For this reason, vacant property tends to be a "hard sell." In addition, potential buyers of vacant property assume that the seller is financially disabled and therefore leap at the opportunity to kick the cripple. Their instincts are usually correct. Vacant property is more likely to attract ridiculously low offers and sellers of vacant property are more likely to accept them.

The solution is to take preventive action to avoid this situation by pricing your home correctly and giving yourself enough time to effect a sale. Assuming this hasn't been done, the alternative is not leaving the home totally vacant. This doesn't mean you have to continue to live there.

No family uses all of their furniture at all times, therefore most sellers can quite easily leave some pieces behind for the sake of appearance and ultimate salability. This works.

CYCLES

All economic activity is subject to cycles. These ups and downs or peaks and troughs involve periods of expansion, contraction, recession and revival. Real estate is affected by three types of cycles: the business, seasonal and neighborhood cycles. The bottoms of these cycles are good or bad depending on whether you are the buyer or seller. The good news is that all three are predictable. What is not predictable in the business and neighborhood cycle is the length and magnitude of the peaks and troughs. The business cycle seems to bottom every fifth year (this is not a prophecy) and the solution for the seller is not to sell during this period. But this doesn't solve the problem for the seller, who, due to a job transfer or other special situation, is forced to sell during bad times.

The good thing about bad times is that they are never totally bad. Homes sell on Christmas Eve, during a recession and in a declining neighborhood and the trick is to make your property one of them.

The easiest and most recommended solution is to lower the price of the property. This is in keeping with the theory that everything will sell if the price is low enough. This is too easy. The best solution is a little more complicated. To begin with, in bad times it is essential that your property get more exposure. Therefore, I think the services of a real estate agency are most important.

Secondly, it is in your interest to expand your market. Lowering the price does expand your market to include more buyers but not to a great degree. A better idea is to offer a carpeting or painting allowance as explained in Chapter 4. This technique may even include raising the price! While a price reduction is helpful, the same reduction in the buyer's down payment is at least five times more helpful, and keep in mind, during a business cycle, down-payment requirements are always higher.

And finally, more attention must be paid to painting, decorating and minor repairs than at other times. Low periods bring out more discriminating buyers.

THE TWO-HOME SITUATION

Many homeowners find themselves in a situation of having to fulfill their contractual obligation to buy a second home without having sold the first. Owning two homes concurrently is expensive, and if the homeowner needs his equity from his first home to meet the down-payment requirements of the second, it is also downright awkward.

Other than delaying the closing of the second home or a default with its subsequent loss of earnest money, the only solution is interim financing.

An interim loan is a short-term loan—generally for three months and renewable—which allows the buyer to meet the down-payment requirements of his new home. The principal and interest on an interim loan is due in full at the end of the loan period or, in other words, there is no monthly payment to worry about.

This, of course, puts the homeowner in the position of being liable for three loans—two mortgage loans and the interim loan. It's still not an enviable position but it prevents a default and allows the buyer to buy his new home, thereby making the best of a bad situation.

A FEW COMMENTS ABOUT FINANCING

There are a number of financing options open to the home buyer or investor. However, the availability of specific types of financing is contingent upon many factors. For example, at this writing the availability of a reverse annuity mortgage in my market is virtually nonexistent. When money is "tight" (when banks and savings and loans associations are short on loanable funds) second mortgages, mortgages on vacation property and certain types of investment loans become hard to find. In addition, many states have interest ceilings or usury laws which prohibit banks from charging interest in excess of a certain percentage. If the money market demands a return in excess of the state usury law then conventional mortgage money disappears.

I have found that, in even the worst of markets, money is still available. It may, however, take a great deal of work to find it. Making 25 telephone calls to various lenders may not be enough. You can expect to pay a higher interest rate and be required to switch your checking and savings account to your new lender.

There is always money around seeking an investment but sometimes it's hard to locate.

A FEW REMARKS ABOUT LYING

My research into lying shows that 75 percent of the lies told have their origin in good manners. These lies are the trademarks of civilized man. I discount them. I concern myself only with the 25 percent whose object is only to damage. And yet, it's not enough to recognize a lie when told. A lie must be interpreted. Why was the lie told, for what advantage to the liar and, most of all, for what disadvantage to you?

Lying is ancient, useful, disgusting, universal, varied, hard to interpret, essential, dangerous, productive, humorous, instinctive and, if you know the ropes, advantageous to you.

A lie can be conveyed visually, orally, behaviorally or statistically. The form is not important although the statistical lie is the most dangerous as it has the appearance of logic.

When a politician promises "tax reform" he means a tax increase, when he promises a tax increase for the rich he means a tax increase for you, a "viable alternative" means one more expensive and counterproductive government program, etc. Buyers lie, sellers lie, tenants lie and real estate salesmen "puff." Your job is to keep from getting screwed by the lie, and I don't mean the caressing friction of fornication.

There is not enough paper under the firmament to discuss every conceivable real estate lie. I will discuss only one. It's your job to interpret it to your particular situation.

PROBLEM I

An apartment-building data sheet indicates:
1. Taxes: $2,200
2. Heater is 5 years old
3. New roof
4. Full occupancy
5. Operating expenses: $3,000

Solution

1. Taxes are a public record. Before buying the building, check with your local assessor to confirm the figure.

2. Have a heating man give you the facts.

3. Observe. Look for leaks. Ask to see the bill.

4. At closing of all income properties (apartment buildings, office buildings, stores, etc.) the buyer should insist on a "rent confirmation" from the tenants. This under-used document requires the seller to furnish a written, signed statement from each tenant describing the status of the rent, amount of security deposit and what furnishings belong to the tenant and owner.

5. Ask to see the canceled checks.

6. A great deal more information can be gathered by a personal and confidential discussion with a few tenants.

Real estate is bought on a "buyer beware" basis. It is the *buyer's* responsibility to know the property (i.e., taxes). In many cases, actual fraud is indistinguishable from aggressive salesmanship and for this reason it is expensive and difficult to prove in court.

In a larger sense, you can travel through life assuming that all men are honest or all men are dishonest. If you believe in the former, sooner or later you will be reduced to penury.

It is characteristic of liars that they don't enjoy being discovered. When they are, they usually become accommodating, oozing, gracious, pliant, guilt-ridden, servile, friendly and, in many other ways, useful to you. *Use them.*

BRIBING

Zoning ordinances, environmental regulations, building codes, property taxes, condominium conversion ordinances and many other municipally administered real estate-related laws are absolutely essential for orderly growth and public safety. However, no law can be considered good when it is expanded to the irrational and selectively applied.

In many markets these laws are outmoded, contradictory, vindictive, impossible to comply with, used as a threat, antigrowth, unimaginative, excessively complex, protective of special interests and retardants to progress and productivity. And yet, land is zoned and developed, buildings are built, construction efficiencies are gradually introduced into the market and all these things occur at ever higher prices. What a paradox.

All of this is made possible by the "drop." This is a fact. Only a cabbage thinks otherwise. Some years ago a Chicago builder stated that 10 percent of his bid price reflected payoffs to city officials.

And yet, screaming about the "injustice of it all" is nothing more than a demonstration of poor sportsmanship. Bribing, prostitution and the evils of drink are unpurgeable camp followers of man's march into the millennium.

It is important to understand that the politician/bureaucrat views these funds as being redirected to a higher purpose—the financial well-being of himself or his political party. It should be the purpose of the investor not to harm the public but only to get on with his endeavor.

Tradition and procedure vary from one locality to another. For example, buying a gross of overpriced number-four pencils from the building inspector's brother-in-law is standard. In some markets you are expected to make the proposal while in others the public official pops the question. The degree of subtlety involved depends on the man and the situation.

There are few universal rules regarding this sort of unpleasantness but the following are general tips:

1. Cost out the favor. This ensures that you won't overpay. "Overtipping" spoils them and ruins it for everybody.

2. Don't align yourself too closely with any one political party. Be cordial to both of them. It's an insurance policy against scandal.

3. If you are unsure of yourself and the deal is large enough, hire a local attorney with clout. In addition to putting a veneer of legality on this business, he is able to insulate you from any future mess.

4. Make sure you "touch" the right man. Don't mistake the promisor for the doer. A misjudgment here leads to a tear-filled night. This is another reason why an attorney, familiar with the local power structure, may be essential.

5. Keep your mouth shut.

COPING

Problems occur throughout a real estate investor's life but they very rarely rise above the disconcerting. Leaking faucets, past-due rent, unforeseen repairs and so many other minor problems have a way of being taken too seriously by many investors. Losing your sense of humor over small things is always counterproductive and I suggest you seek an antidote in mirth. True despair is nothing more than the realization that what your tenants say about you is true and I can't see one reason why you should give the sons-of-bitches the satisfaction.

REAL ESTATE AND THE ENERGY PLOT

The fuel policies of national governments have and will continue to make fossil fuels relatively precious and it's hard to think of any other commodity whose effect on our lives is so universal. Real estate, of course, will be affected. Precisely how and to what extent remain to be seen; however, a few guesses can be made.

We may see an acceleration of the trend toward the more energy-efficient housing concepts—condominiums and town houses—an improvement in energy-efficient home design, the development of more efficient heating systems, the growth of public transportation, the decrease in popularity of the more far-out suburbs or the increased popularity of the neighborhood shopping center. These and other market phenomena may occur and the mix is uncertain. The only thing that is important is the investor's ability to adjust.

WORLD ECONOMIC COLLAPSE

In our age complete economic collapse is an alternative. A deep and prolonged depression would bring with it a political collapse, destruction of the social order and total chaos. The good news is that your real estate problems will be forever solved since the right to own private property would be abolished in the process. I suspect the typical investor's problems would then be to keep out of the way of the ensuing roving bands of Visagoths.

Fortunately, the solution to this problem, like nuclear war, is the simplest of all—not nearly as complex as trying to sell a vacant home.

Don't think about it.

THE BEST WAY TO AVOID PROBLEMS

There is nothing wrong with being an amateur in any particular field. It may even be a sign of good breeding. There is, however, something wrong with an amateur considering himself a pro. This type of attitude marks you as someone who can't read without moving his lips. Bankers, appraisers, attorneys, real estate salesmen, architects, civil engineers, property managers, accountants, general contractors and an assortment of tradesmen, sooner or later, play an important role in the investor's life. Employing these professionals is the best way I know of avoiding problems. Their services also complement the investor's knowledge, thereby ensuring the success of any venture.

Each of these professions stand ready to offer a litany of horror stories of what can happen to you if you don't listen to them, I, therefore, won't get involved. However, the most important thing to remember is that their fees represent only a few percentage points of the transaction or project and are, in most cases, money well spent.

THE REAL ESTATE BUSINESS

Everyone, at some time, wants to write a book, have an affair and sell real estate. And therein lies the problem with these three endeavors. Because real estate is the only one that allows for a part-time commitment, it has become the most crowded.

The real estate business has changed dramatically in the last six years. The growth in the number of offices and salesmen has been phenomenal but the most significant change has been the emergence of the nationally franchised offices. This franchise concept is doing for the real estate business what it did for the hamburger and the "mystery sauce" is "name recognition."

It is felt that within five years 75 percent of residential home sales will be controlled by fewer than ten big national companies. This is a startling prediction for a business always considered local in nature and therefore resistant to bigness.

Local brokers, for several thousand dollars, join a national franchise. In return the broker and his salesmen receive training, sophisticated promotional material and most of all—through national advertising—instant name recognition. And it is this name recognition that is the cutting edge.

In this way the franchise concept has been able to join the advantages of bigness with the necessary local characteristics of real estate.

There are variations of the franchise theme but all have bigness as a goal. This has to be expected since home sales alone account for $200 billion in annual gross sales with commission being about $12 billion. By comparison, the stock-market trades also account for $200 billion but with commission of only about $500 million.

THE BASEMENT

The full basement (six feet or more below ground) is rapidly becoming a museum piece. The development of the clothes dryer and more compact home heater have now made the basement a very expensive hole in the ground.

At one time, basements were essential as areas to hang laundry during bad weather. They were also necessary to accommodate coal bins or heaters larger than circus wagons. The modern heater is now a closet item. More recently they were "finished" and called rec rooms. The popularity of the first-floor family room has, however, made serving chip and dip in a basement a part of fifties nostalgia.

And finally, the basement as storage area no longer makes sense as modern home design provides plenty of attic or garage storage. If you find this inadequate, prefabricated, outdoor sheds may be your answer.

If you still think that basements should be made Article XI of the Bill of Rights, then an understanding of the costs involved may be persuasive. Depending upon size and labor and material costs, a basement option adds between $4,000 and $8,000 to the cost of the average home. It may also add as much as $300 per year to your heating bill. It may flood during a heavy rain, and in time the best of them develop settling cracks which result in seepage.

The alternative to a basement is a much less costly cement platform or crawl space. I believe money saved on a basement can be much better spent on above-ground living area.

If, however, you have a job or hobby which requires a great deal of space, or if you live in an area where tornadoes periodically say hello, then a basement may be for you.

MODULAR CONSTRUCTION

I find the concept of the factory-built home to be the most exciting area of real estate today. It's also called the modular home and, unfortunately, the prefab. By any name it's a special tic with me. It's the first major productivity gain in building since the development of the stick-built method in the nineteenth century.

Its origin, along with the name "prefab," is to be found in World War II. The word "prefab" still invokes the image of a Quonset hut and for this reason should be purged from the language. Construction, design and quality have since been vastly improved, and there is now a large selection of style and floor plan.

In fact, the selection is greater than that of most on-site builders.

The modular home is built in a factory under controlled conditions and uses the efficiences of the assembly line. The home is then transported to the site in sections. A crane places the sections on a site-built concrete platform or foundation.

There is no technological reason why the modular home can't be the dominant housing form in the United States. There are only —you guessed it—institutional reasons. Local government agencies and the "organized labor trust," each for their own self-serving reasons, have conspired to subvert this industry in many areas.

There is one other problem and this lies within the industry. Most factories are located too far from the major housing markets. Therefore, much of the savings of factory construction are "blown" in transportation. I suspect this problem along with certain image difficulties will be solved quicker than the institutional problems.

In spite of these difficulties, I see a bright future for modular construction and my argument is historical. There is no precedent for a better, cheaper way of doing things being suppressed for very long.

I don't believe the modular home to be the ultimate product of the modular construction industry. Someday any building that can be imagined can be built in the factory.

Modular construction is only one of many reasons for the future sustained demand for real estate. Higher family incomes, easier financial methods, tax advantages, inflation psychology, the land lease, energy-efficient design and the increasing popularity of the condominium and town house have been discussed. However, since we are living in an age that requires simple one-word answers to very complex questions, then here it is. The demand and therefore the investment potential of real estate will be sustained co-econo-judico-politico-eco-techno-thermo-socio-chemo-psycho-petro-taxico proletarianistically.

IN DEFENSE OF ARITHMETIC

When the dust settles on Ponzi's world, historians will argue about the cause. It could be the tendency of man to go to extremes, fluoride, the Democratic Party, television, the Maryknolls, rampant iconoclasm, the three-martini lunch, Proposition 13, moral cowardice, the elevation of guilt to virtue, the demotion of equality to egalitarianism, the nattering nabobs of negativism, the nitwit ninnies of nihilism, the know-nothing nose pickers of Nepal, Salt II, cyclamates, sugar, baksheesh, the S.S.T., the yellow peril, the proliferation of any one of 2,127 "isms," Sacco and Vanzetti, the war lost on the playing fields of Harvard, bureaucracy, the politics of gimmee, the misreading of history's lessons. I can't go on. The list of goblins is endless. I cannot sort it out. One longs for a unifier.

Accurate prophecy on such a weighty subject is solely a matter of luck but I'm willing to submit a candidate. My choice is the "willingness of too many people to achieve total freedom by escaping from the strait jacket of arithmetic." This concept can best be illustrated by example.

When mathematics, the heart of the scientific method, is abstracted from medical research, we have the specter of absolutely every work of God or man as a cause of cancer. This is not medicine. It's homeopathy.

When an architect decides to "make a statement" instead of designing a building, he outrages our sense of style, collects a toilet full of awards, gets thirty new commissions and the building collapses. This is not architecture. It's prop design. When an artist violates all sense of spatial relationship, he is not an artist. He is a tie dyer.

When an educator relaxes grade standards to cover his failure, he is not an educator. He's an embezzler.

And so with the politician, who by creating and disguising inflation denies the legitimate aspirations of his people in order to serve the numerology of vote counting.

In the same way, the philosopher becomes the mystic, the journalist becomes the propagandist, the poet becomes the chatterbox, the musician becomes the noisemaker, the civil servant becomes the marplot and they all go "show biz."

Not all professions allow for such a cavalier attitude toward arithmetic. Bullfighting, mountain climbing, auto racing and trapeze work require a great deal of solid geometry. The limits to their fantasies are scribed by death. Arithmetic moderates fantasy. To forget arithmetic here is to be stuffed in a rubber bag.

While the daredevil arts are, by nature, subject to an iron mathematical discipline, the more sedate endeavors are not. The truth is that arithmetical freedom in these callings frequently produces short-term fame and fortune.

As for the investor, bad arithmetic does not lead either to fame or death but the middle ground of bankruptcy.

A nation that forgets its arithmetic is doomed to count its punishments.

YOU ARE THE WORLD'S
ONLY WORTHWHILE CRUSADE

This book is for the player not the puritan. It's not for those anxious to enlist in some just cause and it's not an exposé of anything. There are too many of these and too many wolf-eyed, sweating, bellowing mahatmas ready to lead.

These are nothing but diversions. They can do nothing for you except sidetrack you from working for you and your family's own well-being. Crusades do nothing more than relieve guilt in the cosmopolitan, serve as a hobby for the idle rich, act as a puberty rite for the student, make the politician significant, relieve boredom in the intellectual and make a goat out of you.

It's not a good idea to reform the world. It won't listen. It is, however, a good idea to tailor *your* world to suck out the good.

It is not *my* intention to overwork the epigram although it's a good idea to give it a little exercise. The epigram will not usher in the millennium but it has the potential for great mischief along the way.

All that is necessary is that you understand the game and be willing to play it.

APPENDIX

SAMPLE CONTRACTS

REALTOR

DuPAGE BOARD OF REALTORS
STANDARD RESIDENTIAL SALES CONTRACT

1. BUYER, _____ ; County, _____ ; State _____ agrees to purchase, and

SELLER, _____

Address _____ ; County, _____ ; State _____ agrees to sell to Buyer

at the **PRICE** of _____ Dollars ($ _____),

PROPERTY commonly known as _____

and legally described as follows:

(hereinafter referred to as "the premises")

with approximate lot dimensions of _____

together with all improvements and fixtures, if any, including, but not limited to: All central heating, plumbing and electrical systems and equipment; the hot water heater; central cooling, humidifying and filtering equipment; fixed carpeting; built-in kitchen appliances, equipment and cabinets; water softener (except rental units); existing storm and screen windows and doors; attached shutters, shelving, fireplace screen and ornaments; roof or attic T.V. antenna; all planted vegetation; garage door openers and car units, and the following items of personal property:

All of the foregoing items shall be left on the premises, are included in the sale price, and shall be transferred to the Buyer by a Bill of Sale at the time of closing.

2. THE EARNEST MONEY: Buyer has paid $ _____

(Indicate check and/or note and due date) (and will pay within _____ days the additional sum of $ _____) as earnest money to be applied on the purchase price. The earnest money shall be held by the Listing Broker for the mutual benefit of the parties concerned and upon the closing of the sale, shall be applied first to the payment of any expenses incurred by broker for the Seller in said matter, and second to payment of the broker's sales commission, rendering the overplus, if any, to the Seller.

3. THE CLOSING DATE: _____ , 19 ___ (or on the date, if any, to which said date is extended by reason of paragraph 13) at _____ , or at Buyer's lending institution, if any.

4. POSSESSION: Possession shall be granted to Buyer at 12:01 A.M. on _____ , 19 ___ providing this transaction has closed.

5. THE DEED: Seller shall convey or cause to be conveyed to Buyer (in joint tenancy) or his nominee, by a recordable, stamped general warranty deed with release of homestead rights, good title to the premises subject only to the following "permitted exceptions" if any: (a) General real estate taxes for 19 ___ and subsequent years; (b) Special Assessments confirmed after this contract date; (c) Building, building line and use or occupancy restrictions, conditions and covenants of record; (d) Zoning laws and Ordinances; (e) Easements for public utilities; (f) Drainage ditches, feeders, laterals and drain tile, pipe or other conduit; (g) If the property is other than a detached, single-family home: party walls, party wall rights and agreements; covenants, conditions and restrictions of record; terms, provisions, covenants, and conditions of the declaration of condominium, if any, and all amendments thereto; any easements established by or implied from the said declaration of condominium or amendments thereto, of any; limitations and conditions imposed by the Illinois Condominium Property Act, if applicable; installments of assessments due after the date of closing and easements established pursuant to the declaration of condominium

6. FINANCING CONDITION: This Contract is subject to the condition that within _____ days from the date hereof, the Buyer shall secure, or there shall be made available to the Buyer a written commitment for a loan to be secured by a mortgage or trust deed on the property in the amount of $_____ or such lesser sum as Buyer accepts, with interest not to exceed _____ years.

_____ % per annum, said loan to be repaid in monthly installments over a period of _____ years.

If after the Buyer has submitted a true loan application and otherwise made every reasonable effort to procure a loan commitment from any source made available to him and has been unable to do so, and he serves written notice thereof upon the Seller or his agent within the time specified herein for securing such commitment, then this contract shall become null and void and all monies paid by the Buyer hereunder shall be refunded. IN THE EVENT THE BUYER DOES NOT SERVE NOTICE OF FAILURE TO PROCURE SAID LOAN COMMITMENT UPON SELLER AS HEREIN PROVIDED, THEN THIS CONTRACT SHALL CONTINUE IN FULL FORCE AND EFFECT WITHOUT ANY LOAN CONTINGENCIES. Buyer shall be allowed a reasonable time prior to closing to have a Mortgage or Trust Deed placed of record, and to arrange for access to the proceeds thereof, and any delays caused by Buyer's lending institution in ordering a Commitment for Title Insurance required under paragraph 13 hereof shall not constitute a default by the Seller. Seller shall allow reasonable inspection of the premises by the Buyer (and his financing agent) and furnish any pertinent information requested by them.

7. SURVEY: Prior to closing date Seller shall deliver to Buyer or his agent a spotted survey of the premises, certified by a licensed surveyor, having all corners staked and showing all improvements existing as of this contract date, and all easements and building lines. (In the event the premises is a condominium, only a copy of the pages showing said premises on the recorded survey attached to the Declaration of Condominium shall be required.)

8. SELLER'S REPRESENTATIONS: Seller represents: (a) that he has received no notice of any Ordinance or Building Code violation or pending special assessment from any governmental body in connection with the premises; and (b) that all equipment and appliances to be conveyed, including but not limited to the following, are in operating condition: all mechanical equipment; heating and cooling equipment; water heaters and softeners; septic, plumbing, and electrical systems; kitchen equipment remaining with the premises and any miscellaneous mechanical personal property to be transferred to the Buyer. Upon the Buyer's request, the Seller shall demonstrate to the Buyer or his representative all said equipment and upon receipt of written notice of deficiency shall promptly and at his expense correct the deficiency. IN THE ABSENCE OF WRITTEN NOTICE OF ANY DEFICIENCY FROM THE BUYER PRIOR TO THE CLOSING IT SHALL BE CONCLUDED THAT THE CONDITION OF THE ABOVE EQUIPMENT IS SATISFACTORY TO THE BUYER AND THE SELLER SHALL HAVE NO FURTHER RESPONSIBILITY WITH REFERENCE THERETO.

9. COMMISSION: Seller agrees that _____
Listing Broker, brought about this sale and agrees to pay them a Broker's commission as agreed.

10. COOPERATING BROKER: _____

11. OTHER TERMS AND CONDITIONS: This contract is subject to the Terms and Conditions set forth on the reverse side hereof, which are expressly understood to be a part of this contract.

THE PRINTED MATTER OF THIS CONTRACT HAS BEEN PREPARED UNDER THE SUPERVISION OF THE DUPAGE BOARD OF REALTORS AND THE DUPAGE COUNTY BAR ASSOCIATION. HOWEVER, THE PARTIES ARE CAUTIONED THAT THIS IS A LEGALLY BINDING CONTRACT. IF THE TERMS ARE NOT UNDERSTOOD PLEASE SEEK LEGAL COUNSEL BEFORE SIGNING IT.

DATED: _____ , 19 ____ .

_____ _____
Buyer   Seller

_____ _____
Buyer   Seller

12. LEGAL DESCRIPTION: If a complete legal description is not included herein, it may be inserted by either party hereto.

13. TITLE: (a) At least one (1) business day prior to the closing date, Seller shall furnish or cause to be furnished to Buyer at Seller's expense an Owner's Duplicate Certificate of Title issued by the Registrar of Titles and a Special Tax and Lien Search or a commitment issued by a title insurance company licensed to do business in Illinois, to issue an owner's title insurance policy on the current form of American Land Title Association Owner's Policy (or equivalent policy) in the amount of the purchase price covering the date hereof, subject only to: (1) the general exceptions contained in the policy, unless the contract price is $100,000.00 or less and the real estate is improved with a single family dwelling or an apartment building of four or fewer residential units, (2) the "permitted exceptions" set forth in paragraph 5, (3) title exceptions pertaining to liens or encumbrances of a definite or ascertainable amount, which may be removed by the payment of money at the time of closing (an amount sufficient to secure the release of such title exceptions shall be deducted from the proceeds of sale due Seller at closing), and (4) acts done or suffered by, or judgments against Buyer, or those claiming by, through or under Buyer. (b) If the title commitment discloses unpermitted exceptions, the Seller shall have thirty (30) days from the date of delivery thereof to have the said exceptions waived, or to have the title insurer commit to insure against loss or damage that may be caused by such exceptions and the closing date shall be delayed, if necessary, during said 30 day period to allow Seller time to have said exceptions waived. If the Seller fails to have unpermitted exceptions waived, or, in the alternative, to obtain a commitment for title insurance specified above as to such exceptions, within the specified time, the Buyer may terminate the contract between the parties, or may elect, upon notice to the Seller within ten (10) days after the expiration of the thirty (30) day period, to take the title as it then is, with the right to deduct from the purchase price, liens or encumbrances of a definite or ascertainable amount. If the Buyer does not so elect, the contract between the parties shall become null and void, without further action of the parties, and all monies paid by Buyer hereunder shall be refunded. (c) Every title commitment which conforms with subparagraph "a" shall be conclusive evidence of good title therein shown, as to all matters insured by the policy, subject only to special exceptions therein stated.

14. AFFIDAVIT OF TITLE: Seller shall furnish Buyer at closing with an Affidavit of Title, covering the date of closing, subject only to those permitted special exceptions set forth in paragraph 5, and unpermitted exceptions, if any, as to which the title insurer commits to extend insurance in the manner specified in paragraph 13. In the event that the contract between the parties calls for title to be conveyed by a Trustee's Deed, the Affidavit of Title required to be furnished by Seller shall be signed by the beneficiary or beneficiaries of said Trust.

15. ESCROW CLOSING: At the election of Seller or Buyer, upon notice to the other party not less than five (5) days prior to the closing date, the sale shall be closed through an Escrow with a title company licensed to do business in the State of Illinois, in accordance with the general provisions of a deed and money escrow agreement consistent with the terms of this contract. Upon creation of such an Escrow, anything in this contract between the parties to the contrary notwithstanding, payment of the purchase price and delivery of the Deed shall be made through the Escrow; and, if no broker is involved in the transaction, the earnest money shall be deposited in the Escrow. The cost of the Escrow shall be divided equally between the Seller and the Buyer, except that the Buyer shall pay the money lender's escrow charges.

16. PRORATIONS: (a) General real estate taxes shall be prorated as of the closing date on the basis of the tax assessor's latest assessed value.

of the closing date.

17. CLEAN CONDITION: Seller agrees to leave the premises in broom clean condition. All refuse and personal property not to be conveyed to Buyer shall be removed from the premises at Seller's expense before the date of occupancy.

18. PERFORMANCE: Time is of the essence of this contract. Should Buyer fail to perform this contract, then at the option of the Seller and upon written notice to the Buyer, the earnest money shall be forfeited by the Buyer as liquidated damages and the contract shall thereupon become null and void and the Seller shall have the right if necessary and applicable, to re-enter and take possession of the premises aforesaid, and all right in and title to said premises and any and all improvements made upon said premises by the Buyer shall vest in the Seller.

19. NOTICES: All notices required to be given under this contract shall be construed to mean notice in writing signed by or on behalf of the party giving the same, and the same may be served upon the other party or his agent personally or by certified or registered mail, return receipt requested, to the parties at the address set forth herein.

20. The covenants, warranties and other provisions of this contract shall survive the closing of this transaction. However nothing contained in paragraph 8 shall be construed as a warranty that the items therein mentioned will remain in good repair beyond the date of closing or the date on which possession is delivered to Buyer, whichever shall first occur.

21. In the event the premises is a townhouse or condominium, Seller shall furnish Buyer a statement from the Board of Managers, Treasurer or Managing Agent of the condominium association certifying payment of assessments for condominium common expenses; and if applicable, proof of waiver or termination of any right of first refusal or general option contained in the declaration of condominium together with any other documents required by the declaration of condominium or by-laws thereto as a precondition to the transfer of ownership.

22. In the event that, prior to closing, the subject premises shall be destroyed or damaged by fire or other casualty to an extent that the cost of repair thereof exceeds 10% of the purchase price set forth herein; or in the event any portion of the subject premises shall be taken by governmental action through condemnation, then, at the option of either party hereto, this contract shall be declared null and void and the Buyer shall be entitled to a return of all monies paid hereunder.

THE PRINTED MATTER OF THIS CONTRACT HAS BEEN PREPARED UNDER THE SUPERVISION OF THE DUPAGE BOARD OF REALTORS AND THE DUPAGE COUNTY BAR ASSOCIATION. HOWEVER, THE PARTIES ARE CAUTIONED THAT THIS IS A LEGALLY BINDING CONTRACT. IF THE TERMS ARE NOT UNDERSTOOD PLEASE SEEK LEGAL COUNSEL BEFORE SIGNING IT.

Form #100 Copyright 1959 Rev. 3/78

EXCLUSIVE LISTING CONTRACT

STANDARD RESIDENTIAL EXCLUSIVE LISTING CONTRACT • DuPage Board of Realtors

REALTOR

TO: _____

(Listing Realtor's Name and Address)

In consideration of your acceptance of the terms hereof and your promise to use your efforts to sell the real estate known as

(Address) _____

(Legal) _____

I give you the exclusive right to sell or exchange this property to qualified purchasers regardless of race, color, creed, national origin, sex, or physical disability; and to advertise and show the property; and to share this property with the Realtor members of the _____

Multiple Listing Service of which you are a member beginning 12:01 A.M., Day _____ Month _____ Year _____ and terminating 11:59 P.M. Day _____ Month _____ Year _____ .

THE LISTING PRICE shall be $ _____ .

TITLE is in my name and/or _____ .

POSSESSION shall be given _____ .

All inquiries about this listing made to me will be immediately referred to you, the Realtor.

All central heating, plumbing and electrical systems and equipment; the hot water heater; central cooling, humidifying and filtering equipment; fixed carpeting; built-in kitchen appliances, equipment and cabinets; water softener (except rental units); existing storm and screen windows and doors; attached shutters, shelving, fireplace screen and ornaments; roof or attic T.V. antenna; all planted vegetation; garage door openers and car units, together with all improvements and fixtures, if any, shall be left on the premises, are included in the sale price, and shall be transferred to the Buyer by a Bill of Sale at the time of closing. The following items shall also be left on the premises and conveyed to Buyer at time of closing: _____

All equipment remaining with the property is paid for, belongs to me, the owner, and will be in operating condition at the time of closing, except for the following _____

I have no knowledge of any assessments or special taxes for improvements or lien for improvements, either of record or in process pending, applicable to the property listed herein and should I, in the future, receive any notice thereof, I agree to notify you immediately.

All taxes and all usually prorated expenses shall be prorated to the date of closing. The Realtor's sole duty is to effect a sale of the property, and you, the Listing Realtor, and members of the Multiple Listing Service to which you belong, are not charged with the custody of the property, its management, maintenance, upkeep or repair. In real estate sales, Illinois law allows brokers to prepare the sale contract but not other legal documents required to close the sale. THEREFORE I AGREE TO FURNISH OR HAVE MY ATTORNEY FURNISH ALL OTHER LEGAL DOCUMENTS NECESSARY TO CLOSE THE SALE.

You are hereby authorized to display a "For Sale" sign(s) on the property. In the event of a sale, a "Sold" sign(s) may be displayed on the property for a reasonable length of time. You are authorized to affix a keybox to the premises, and any Realtor or salesperson associated with the Multiple Listing Service(s) to which you belong shall have the right, through use of said keybox, to show the premises at any reasonable time, provided the owner is absent.

As owner, I declare I have not added to nor disposed of any part of the property, or gained any easements in favor of or against the property not disclosed in the Title Guaranty Policy except as stated herein. Prior to closing I agree to furnish at my expense an Owner's Duplicate Certificate of Title issued by the Registrar of Titles and a Special Tax and Lien Search or a title insurance commitment for an Owner's Title Insurance Policy in the amount of the sale price, showing good title in the owner's name and brought down to date of sale. Prior to closing I agree to furnish a spotted survey prepared by a licensed surveyor, having all corners staked and all improvements existing as of the sale contract date shown.

If any sale or exchange is made by you, by myself or by anyone else during this listing period, or if sold within _____ after the termination of this agreement to anyone who has viewed the premises within the period of this listing, or any extension thereof, I agree to pay you a commission of _____ on the full sale price, including any encumbrances.

* A commission shall be deemed to have been earned at such time as a sales contract or exchange is executed, or an option has been exercised, involving the subject property. Said commission shall be paid at the time of closing or settlement. If there is a default of the contract of sale involving the subject property, then the commission shall be paid following the default or, if contested, upon settlement or court adjudication between the parties.

Although the purpose of this Listing Contract is to bring about a sale or exchange of the property, if the property is rented within the listing period, then I, the owner, agree to pay you a rental commission of _____ .

If the tenant to whom the property is rented later purchases this property by virtue of an option, or for any other reason, then I agree to pay you a sales commission of _____ on the full sale price, including any encumbrances.

THE EARNEST MONEY shall be held by you, the listing broker, and upon the closing of the sale or upon forfeiture of the sale contract, applied first to the payment of any expense incurred on my behalf in the sale, and second to payment of the broker's sales commission to you, rendering the overplus, if any, to me, the seller.

It is understood and agreed that you will submit pertinent information concerning this listed property to the Multiple Listing Service(s) of which you are a member. It is further understood that you will promptly furnish to such Multiple Listing Service(s) notice of all changes of information concerning listed property as agreed by me, and that upon completion of a fully executed sales agreement on listed property, you will notify the Multiple Listing Service(s) of said sale and authorize the dissemination of sales information including selling price to the participants of said Multiple Listing Service(s) prior to closing of transaction. No alterations in the terms hereof shall be valid or binding unless made in writing and signed by the parties hereto.

Accepted (office) _____ OWNER _____

By (Realtor) _____

Date _____

Inspection Date _____ Day _____

EQUAL OPPORTUNITY IN HOUSING

WHITE - LISTER
YELLOW - SELLER
PINK   - MULTIPLE LISTINGS

NEW 9-78

GLOSSARY OF
REAL ESTATE TERMS

ABSTRACT OF TITLE. A history of a parcel of property including all recorded documents from the original grant to present. Includes all conveyances and encumbrances.

ACCELERATED DEPRECIATION. A depreciation schedule occuring faster than the straight-line rate.

ACCELERATION CLAUSE. Gives the lender the right, upon default, to immediately demand payment of its mortgage in full.

ACRE. A land measure consisting of 43,560 square feet, 160 square rods or 4,840 square yards.

AFFIDAVIT OF TITLE. A written, sworn statement in which the seller certifies that since title examination there have been no judgments, bankruptcies, divorces, unrecorded deeds or repairs and improvements that have not been paid for.

AGENT. One who acts for another such as a real estate broker acting on behalf of another.

AIR RIGHTS. The right to use the air space above property, generally used in connection with condominiums.

AMENITIES. Those improvements to land which increase enjoyment rather than the needs of the resident (scenic beauty, pool, etc.).

AMORTIZATION. Debt repayment in equal installments over a fixed period of time.

APPRECIATION. Any increase in value whether due to improvement of the area, inflation or the elimination of negative factors.

"AS IS" CONDITION. The buyer or tenant acceptance of property in the condition at the time of sale or lease including all negative features.

ASSESSED VALUE. The value placed on property by the assessor for tax purposes.

ASSUMPTION. A financing method in which the buyer assumes the seller's debt liability.

BI-LEVEL. Split level.

BILL OF SALE. The instrument by which personal property is transferred.

BUILDING CODES. City or county requirements which set minimum standards of construction, including design and materials, in order to protect public safety and health.

BUILDING PERMIT. A document issued by a local government allowing the construction of a building.

CAPITAL GAINS. The difference between the buying and selling price (less transaction costs and improvements) of a capital asset.

CAPITALIZATION. Determining value of income property by dividing the annual net income by the rate of return desired by the average investor. $\dfrac{\text{Income}}{\text{Rate}} = \text{Value}$

CASH FLOW. The actual cash the investor receives after deducting operating expenses and debt repayment.

CAVEAT EMPTOR. Buyer beware.

CEMENT BLOCK. A hollow cement building block.

CHAIN OF TITLE. The chronological order of owners of a particular property.

CHATTEL. Personal Property.

CIRCUIT BREAKER. (1) An electrical device replacing the fuse—protects against electrical overload; (2) a type of property tax relief of principal benefit to the elderly.

CLAPBOARD. Narrow, horizontal boards with one edge thicker than the other; used as siding.

CLOSING COSTS. Transaction costs in buying or selling real estate (i.e., loan fees, appraisal fees, survey fees, title fees).

CLOSING STATEMENT. A computation on the day of closing of all financial adjustments between buyer and seller used to determine the net amount the buyer must pay the seller.

COMMON AREA. That portion of land or buildings owned in common by the owners of condominiums.

COMMON BRICK. Untreated brick having no uniform color.

COMPARABLES. Properties similar to the one being appraised and used as an indication of value.

CONDEMNATION. The government taking of private property for public use with compensation to the owner.

CONSIDERATION. Something of value which induces one to enter into a contract.

CONSTRUCTION LOAN. A short-term financing of real estate construction.

CONSTRUCTIVE EVICTION. Not actual eviction but any action by the landlord which makes the property uninhabitable to the tenant.

CONTINGENCY. A specific event which must occur before a contract is considered binding. (The buyer's obligation is contingent upon obtaining financing.)

CONVENTIONAL MORTGAGE. Any mortgage which is not insured by a government agency such as FHA or VA.

CONVERSION. The changing of an apartment or hotel to a condominium.

CORPORATION. A body of persons granted a charter legally recognizing them as a separate entity having its own rights, privileges and liabilities distinct from those of its members.

CORRELATION. The weighted use of the three different appraisal methods to arrive at an estimate of value.

COUNTER OFFER. An offer made in response to an offer.

C.R.V. (Certificate of Reasonable Value). An appraisal for the purpose of securing a VA-insured loan.

DECLINING BALANCE METHOD OF DEPRECIATION. Depreciation by a fixed annual percentage of the balance after deducting each yearly depreciation amount.

DEED. A document which transfers ownership of real estate.

DEFAULT. Failure to meet an obligation when due (monthly mortgage payment).

DEPRECIATION. Loss of value due to (1) physical deterioration (wear and tear); (2) functional depreciation or obsolescence, or (3) economic obsolescence (surrounding market).

EARNEST MONEY. An amount deposited by a buyer at the time of signing a contract. This money is used as all or part of the down payment or if the buyer defaults is forfeited to the seller.

EASEMENT. The right to use the property of another for a specific purpose—commonly given to utilities.

ECONOMIC LIFE. The profitable life of an improvement—generally not as long as the physical life.

ENCROACHMENT. Any structure or some portion of it which extends beyond the lot line (boundary) of the owner onto the property of another.

EQUITY. The value which an owner has over and above his mortgage balance.

ESCALATION CLAUSE. A clause in a lease which provides for a future increase in rent.

EXCLUSIVE AGENCY LISTING. Same as an exclusive listing; however, the owner reserves the right to sell his own property without a commission obligation.

EXCLUSIVE LISTING. A listing contract under which the owner appoints a real estate broker as his only agent for a fixed period of time to sell his property.

EXECUTION. To sign, seal and deliver an instrument.

FACE BRICK. A treated exterior brick, usually glossy and of even quality.

FAIR MARKET VALUE. The price a ready, willing and informed seller will accept and a ready, willing, able and informed buyer will pay for a property assuming the property is exposed for a reasonable length of time.

FEDERAL SAVINGS AND LOAN ASSOCIATION. A federally chartered institution for savings and real estate loans under the regulation of the Federal Home Loan Bank Board.

FHA (FEDERAL HOUSING ADMINISTRATION). Insures low down-payment loans made by approved lenders in accordance with its regulations.

FIDUCIARY RELATIONSHIP. A relationship of trust and confidence such as between attorney and client or broker and seller.

FIRST MORTGAGE. A mortgage which has priority as a lien over all other mortgages.

FIXTURE. Personal property attached permanently to a structure so that it is considered real estate.

FLASHING. Sheet metal used to prevent water seepage such as around a chimney.

FLOOD PLAIN. Land adjoining a river which would flood if the river overflowed its banks.

FORECLOSURE. A court action by the lender requiring the sale of the debtor's real estate in order to satisfy the mortgage or other lien.

FRONT FOOTAGE. The measurement along the front of the property bordering on the street.

GAMBREL ROOF. A ridged roof, each side having two slopes, the lower of which is more inclined.

GENERAL CONTRACTOR. Contracts for the construction of an entire building rather than a portion of it. Subcontractors (plumbing, electrical, etc.) are responsible to him and he is responsible for payment to them.

GRADE. The degree of the slope of land.

GRANTEE. Buyer.

GRANTOR. Seller.

GROSS INCOME MULTIPLIER. A figure which when multiplied by the gross annual income will give the market value.

GROSS LEASE. A lease in which the landlord pays all costs of ownership (repairs, taxes, insurance and operating expenses).

HIGHEST AND BEST USE. That use of land which will yield the greatest return and thereby develop the highest land value.

HIP ROOF. A roof with four sloping sides that rise to a ridge.

IMPROVEMENTS. Buildings, streets, sewers or sidewalks.

JOINT TENANTS. Two or more owners of a parcel of land so named on the deed. Upon the death of a joint tenant, his interest passes to the surviving joint tenant or joint tenants by the right of survivorship.

LAND CONTRACT. An installment contract for the sale of real estate whereby the seller retains legal title until paid in full.

LESSEE. Tenant.

LESSOR. Landlord.

LEVERAGE. The use of financing to allow a small cash down payment to purchase a large investment.

LIEN. The right of a creditor to have his debt paid by the sale of the debtor's property.

LIMITED PARTNERSHIP. A type of syndication consisting of one or more general partners who conduct the business and are responsible for losses and one or more limited partners contributing capital and liable only for that amount contributed.

LOCAL GOVERNMENT. City or county government authority.

MANSARD ROOF. A four-sided roof, each side having two separate slopes; the lower slope is steeper than the upper slope.

MARKET DATA APPROACH. An appraisal method which estimates value by comparing actual sales with the property being appraised.

MECHANIC'S LIEN. A lien by unpaid contractors or laborers who have performed work in constructing or repairing a building.

M.G.I.C. (MORTGAGE GUARANTY INSURANCE CORPORATION). A private insurer of conventional loans. Like FHA, the premium is paid by the borrower.

MORTGAGEE. The lender.

MORTGAGE LIFE INSURANCE. A decreasing-term life insurance policy for the approximate amount of the declining balance of a mortgage loan. In the event of the death of the owner, the mortgage is paid.

MORTGAGER. The borrower.

MULTIPLE LISTING. An exclusive listing submitted by a broker to all members of an association giving each an opportunity to sell the property.

NET INCOME. The difference between gross income and operating expenses. May or may not include depreciation.

NET LEASE. A lease requiring the tenant to pay, in addition to rent, other costs of ownership including taxes, insurance, repair and maintenance.

NET WORTH. The difference between the total assets and liabilities of an individual or corporation.

NONBEARING WALL. A wall which does not support a structure but only separates rooms.

NOTE. An instrument of credit attesting to a debt.

OPEN LISTING. A listing which requires the broker to provide a buyer for the owner's property before the owner or any other broker in order to collect a commission.

OPERATING EXPENSES. Costs involved in owning income-producing property such as taxes, insurance, management and utilities.

OPTION. The right to buy or lease property, given for a consideration at an agreed-upon price and terms within a fixed period of time.

ORIEL WINDOW. Similar to a bay window but supported by brackets instead of the foundation.

PARTNERSHIP. An association of two or more persons to carry on as co-owners a business for profit.

PARTY WALL. A wall erected on a property boundary supporting structures on both sides. (Of concern to owners of condominiums and town houses.)

PERCENTAGE LEASE. Allows the owner to collect in addition to a base rental a percentage of the gross or net sales of the retail tenant.

PERCOLATION TEST. A procedure used to test the capability of soil to absorb liquid (for construction and septic systems).

PLANNING COMMISSION. A county or city board which must approve proposed building projects.

PLAT. An aerial-view, drawn map which divides a parcel of land into lots.

POINT. One percent of a mortgage loan. Paid by the seller in FHA and VA loans and paid by the buyer or seller in conventional loans.

POWER OF ATTORNEY. A written instrument authorizing one to act for another.

PRO RATE (PRO RATA). To divide in proportionate shares.

QUIT CLAIM DEED. A conveyance of real estate in which the grantor transfers his interest in real estate, if any, without warranties or obligations.

RAW LAND. Land without water, streets, sidewalks, sewer utilities and which has not been subdivided into lots.

REALTOR. A designation given to a real estate broker who is an active member of a local board of realtors affiliated with the National Association of Realtors.

RECAPTURE. The return of money invested through loan reduction and appreciation. This is realized when the property is sold.

REINFORCED CONCRETE. Concrete strengthened by steel rods or mesh.

RENT CONTROL. A legal maximum on rental price.

REPLACEMENT COST. The current cost of replacing a property with the same utility and amenities.

REVENUE STAMPS. State tax stamps affixed to a deed.

ROW HOUSES. Town houses.

SECOND MORTGAGE. A mortgage loan secured by real estate and ranking after a first mortgage in priority as a lien.

SEPTIC SYSTEM. A sewage disposal system in which waste material is drained into a tank and decomposed bacteriologically.

SKYLIGHT. A window in the roof or ceiling.

SPECIAL ASSESSMENT. A charge against real estate made by local government to cover the proportionate cost of improvements such as streets or sewers.

STRAIGHT-LINE DEPRECIATION. A method of replacing the capital investment of income property by reducing a fixed annual amount from the income over the economic life of the property.

SUBLEASE. A lease in which a tenant re-leases to another tenant.

SYNDICATE. Any group business venture.

TENANCY. A form of real estate ownership by two or more persons. The interests need not be equal and in the event of the death of one owner the other does not inherit his interest.

TERM. A period of time such as for a lease or mortgage.

TITLE. The evidence of the right a person has to ownership and possession of land.

TITLE INSURANCE POLICY. A policy insuring an owner or lender against any loss resulting from defects in the title to land except for stated exceptions.

TOPOGRAPHICAL SURVEY. Survey showing the difference in grade of land.

TRAFFIC COUNT. The number of vehicles or people passing a given point in a given period of time. Used to determine retail business site development.

VA MORTGAGE. A mortgage loan made to a qualified veteran by an authorized lender and guaranteed by the Veterans Administration to limit possible loss by the lender.

VAPOR BARRIER. A moisture-retarding material used on walls to prevent condensation.

VARIANCE. An exception made to a zoning ordinance.

VENEER. Thin sheets of wood or brick over less costly material.

WEATHER STRIPS. Felt or metal strips installed between a door or window and its casing to keep out the elements.

ZONING ORDINANCE. A municipal regulation of land use.

BIBLIOGRAPHY

Appraisal of Real Estate, The. Chicago, Ill.: American Institute of Real Estate Appraisers, 1978.

Britton, James A., and Kerwood, Lewis O. *Financing Income Producing Real Estate.* New York: McGraw-Hill Book Company, 1977.

California Association of Realtors. *How to Convert Apartments to Condominiums.* Los Angeles, 1973; reprinted, 1977.

——*How to Manage Condominium Developments.* Los Angeles, 1976.

Cornwell, Richard E., C.P.M. *The Miniwarehouse: A Guide for Investors and Managers. A Case Study.* Chicago, Ill.: Institute of Real Estate Management, 1975.

Gabriel, Richard F. *Complete Guide to Building a Real Estate Fortune Investing in Older Multiple Dwellings.* Englewood Cliffs, N.J.: Executive Reports Corp., 1977.

Galaty, Fillmore W., Allaway, Wellington J., and Kyle, Robert C. *Modern Real Estate Practice,* 8th edition. Chicago, Ill.: Real Estate Educational Corp., 1978.

Greer, Gaylon E. *The Real Estate Investor and Federal Income Tax.* New York: Ronald Press Publications, 1978.

Hathaway, Frank. *How to Make Money in Rural Real Estate.* Englewood Cliffs, N.J.: Executive Reports Corp., 1975.

Kelly, Edward N. *Practical Apartment Management.* Chicago, Ill.: Institute of Real Estate Management, 1976.

Lion, Edgar and Eng, P. *Shopping Centers—Planning, Development and Administration.* New York: Wiley-Interscience, 1976.

National Association of Home Builders. *Land Development Manual.* Washington, D.C., 1974.

Romney, Keith B. *Condominium Development Guide: Procedures, Analysis, Forms.* Boston, Mass.: Warren and Lamont, 1974.

——*Condominium Development Guide: Cumulative Supplement.* Bos-

INDEX